DASH Diet

100 Delicious DASH Recipes - Including a DASH Diet Guide for Beginners

perceived slight of any individual or organization is purely unintentional.

Contents

Manuscript 1:
DASH Diet
The DASH Diet for Beginners with Delicious DASH Recipes for Weight Loss

Introduction

I want to thank you and commend you for opening the book, "DASH Diet: The DASH Diet For Beginners With Delicious DASH Recipes for Weight Loss".

This book is a guide on how to effectively lose unwanted pounds with the help of the DASH Diet.

The DASH (Dietary Approaches to Stop Hypertension) is a healthy eating plan tailored to help in treating high blood pressure or preventing it in the first place. By encouraging you to reduce your sodium intake as well as consume potassium/calcium/magnesium-rich foods (they help lower blood pressure levels), you decrease your risk of high blood pressure.

You even benefit from reduced risk of getting heart disease, stroke, diabetes, osteoporosis and cancer. The fact that the DASH Diet guides you to making healthier food choices also makes it easier for you to lose weight.

Thanks again for opening this book, I hope you enjoy it!

Chapter 1 – DASH Diet Takeaways To Live By

DASH-Approved Foods

Plenty of vegetables, fruits, whole grains, and low-fat dairy are included in the DASH Diet plan. Other DASH Diet-approved foods you should consume are legumes as well as fish and poultry. The DASH Diet also allows you to have seeds and nuts in small amounts a few times per week. You may also indulge in small amounts of sweets, fats and red meats, so you get to enjoy your food while still keeping your diet low in total fat, saturated fat, and cholesterol.

To ensure that you are losing weight and keeping your blood pressure levels at bay, consider the following recommended servings for different food groups included in your DASH Diet:

1. Vegetables: 4 – 5 daily servings

Go for vegetables that are rich in fiber as well as vitamins and minerals (including magnesium and potassium) such as greens, tomatoes, sweet potatoes, broccoli and carrots. One vegetable serving is equivalent to one-half cup of cut-up vegetables (raw/cooked) or one cup of leafy green veggies (raw). You can increase the number of vegetable servings in your daily diet by being creative in your meal preparations. For example, you may reduce meat by half and then double up on your veggies when making stir-fry.

It helps to not consider vegetables as just side dishes. Know that you can prepare a hearty main dish by simply serving a generous blend of veggies on top of whole wheat noodles or brown rice. You don't even have to be picky about using only fresh vegetables; frozen works just as well in the DASH Diet. Just remember to only choose frozen (or canned) vegetables that are labeled as without added salt or low-sodium.

2. Fruits: 4 – 5 daily servings

Little preparation is needed to make a number of fruits a part of your healthy DASH Diet eating plan. You can easily incorporate fruits into your meals or snacks as they are similar to vegetables in terms of fiber, magnesium, and potassium content (high) as well as fat content (low).

One serving of fruit is equivalent to one medium-sized fruit, one-half cup of fresh/frozen/canned fruit, or four ounces of fruit juice. To get your daily fruit requirement, you can complement your meals with one piece of fruit, have another one for a healthy snack, and finish off with a bowl of fresh fruit dessert topped with a spoonful of plain, low-fat yogurt.

Keep in mind that fruits with pits like apples and pears are best eaten with their peels on. Aside from containing fiber and other healthy nutrients, the edible peels allow these fruits to provide an interesting texture to your recipes. It also helps to consult your doctor about eating grapefruit and other citrus fruits, which may interact with any medications you are taking. And if you must use canned fruits or juices, stick to the "no sugar added" kind.

3. Healthy Fats and Oils: 2 – 3 daily servings

Although fat is essential to your health (it aids your body in absorbing essential vitamins and supports your immune system function), too much of it does increase your risk of becoming obese, having diabetes, and having heart disease.

Your DASH Diet plan will have you aiming for reduced total fat (no more than thirty percent of your daily calories should come from fat) to achieve a healthy balance, which is easier since you are encouraged to focus on monounsaturated fats. One serving of healthy fat is equivalent to one teaspoon of soft margarine, two tablespoons of salad dressing, or one tablespoon of mayonnaise.

Limit your use of meat, cream, whole milk, cheese, butter and eggs, as well as any food made from palm oils, coconut oils, lard and solid shortenings. This will help you keep your daily intake of saturated fat less than 6% of your total daily calories.

Steer clear of fried foods, baked goods, crackers and other processed foods to help you avoid consuming trans fat. It also helps to check food labels when buying salad dressings and margarines – go for those that contain zero trans fat and the least saturated fat.

4. Grains: 6 – 8 daily servings

One serving of grains (including rice, cereal, bread, and pasta) is equivalent to one-half cup of rice/cereal/pasta (cooked), one ounce of cereal (dry), or one slice of bread (whole wheat). Stick to whole grains, which have higher fiber and nutrient content compared to refined grains. You can substitute brown rice for white rice, whole grain bread for white bread, or whole wheat pasta for regular pasta.

Make sure to look for 100% whole grain or whole wheat products, and to keep them in their naturally low-fat state by not adding cream, cheese sauce, or butter to them.

5. Fish, poultry and lean meat: 6 daily servings or fewer

The DASH Diet allows meat in small amounts as it is abundant in protein as well as iron, zinc and B vitamins. Go for lean meat. Limit yourself to up to six ounces daily – this way, you have more room for veggies. Make sure to trim away fat and skin from your meat and poultry before – no frying in fat! –

roasting, grilling, or baking. Reduce your total cholesterol further by eating fish rich in omega-3s such as tuna, salmon and herring.

6. Dairy: 2 – 3 daily servings

It is important to limit your dairy to fat-free or low-fat choices as they mostly contain saturated fat. But because they are rich sources of protein as well as calcium and vitamin D, you can still include them in your DASH Diet. Once dairy serving is equivalent to one cup of 1% milk, one cup of skim milk, one cup of low-fat yogurt, or 1 ½ ounces of cheese (part-skim).

Give your dairy consumption a boost by having frozen yogurt (fat-free or low-fat); sweeten things up by adding fruit. But if you have issues with digesting dairy, go for products that come with lactase (an enzyme that reduces or prevents lactose intolerance symptoms) or that are lactose-free. When eating cheese, remember that even the fat-free ones are not to be consumed in high amounts, as they do contain too much sodium.

7. Legumes, nuts and seeds: 4 – 5 daily servings

Potassium, magnesium and protein can be found in high amounts in lentils, peas, kidney beans, almonds and sunflower seeds. Legumes, seeds and nuts are also rich in fiber as well as phytochemicals that may help protect you against cardiovascular disease and certain cancers. Because they do contain many calories, it is best to have them in small servings and just a few times per week. Remember that one serving is equivalent to one-half cup of peas or beans (cooked), two tablespoons of seeds, or one-third cup of nuts.

Tofu, tempeh, and other soybean-based products can easily replace meat – they are also rich in amino acids, which your body uses to build protein.

You can eat nuts in moderation to benefit from their omega-3s and monounsaturated fat content while not adding to the already-high calories they provide. Use them to add texture to your cereals, salads or stir-fries.

8. Sweets: 5 daily servings or less

When eating the DASH Diet way, there is no need to completely eliminate sweets. The key is to never overindulge: Keep your daily servings down to 5 or less. Remember that one sweets serving is equivalent to one tablespoon of sugar, one tablespoon of jam, one tablespoon of jelly, one-half cup of sorbet, or one cup of lemonade. It will also be best for you to stick to low-fat or fat-free versions of your favorite sweet treats, including low-fat cookies, graham crackers, fruit ices, sorbets, hard candy, and jelly beans.

Tips for Eating the DASH Diet Way

1. Purchase foods that have the words "low sodium," "very low sodium," "sodium-free," or no salt added" clearly spelled out on their labels. Keep in mind that 1 tablespoon of salt gives you two thousand three hundred twenty-five milligrams of sodium. Reading food labels will help you realize that a number of processed foods contain too much sodium. Be wary even of cereals (ready-to-eat), canned veggies, low-fat soups, and deli turkey slices – although they are generally considered healthy, they do contain high amounts of sodium.

2. Instead of salt, make use of sodium-free spices and other flavorings to liven up your food.

3. If you have to use canned foods, make sure to rinse well to lessen the amount of sodium.

4. Skip the addition of salt to the water when cooking hot cereal, rice, or pasta.

5. Foods and beverages that are of the low-sodium kind can seem too bland for your taste. To allow your taste buds some time to adjust, it would be a good idea to gradually include these low-sodium foods to your diet plan while cutting back on your use of table salt.

6. Dining out the DASH Diet way is possible if you make sure that your food is prepared with no added salt or MSG. Also, it pays to watch out for smoked, cured or pickled foods as well as any dish that contains broth or soy sauce – they may be prepared with lots of salt. Use ketchup, mustard, sauces, and other salt-laden condiments sparingly. And avoid the saltshaker at all cost.

7. Make use of DASH Diet-friendly cookware. Use a vegetable steamer when preparing veggies without oil or butter. When sautéing veggies or meat, use nonstick cookware to reduce the amount of butter or oil you have to use. And a garlic press or spice mill will help you avoid using the saltshaker when you want to make your food more flavorful.

Chapter 2 – DASH-Diet Friendly Appetizer and Bread Recipes

To ensure your success in adopting a DASH Diet plan for life while effectively losing weight, it is best to change things gradually. For example, if you are currently eating just 1 to 2 servings of vegetables or fruits per day, consider adding one serving each at lunch and at dinner. If you want to try going only for whole grains, you can begin by replacing 1 to 2 of your usual grains with whole grains.

APPETIZERS

Easy Avocado Dip

Ingredients:
Avocado, ripe, peeled, pitted, mashed (1 piece)
Sour cream, fat-free (1/2 cup)
Hot sauce (1/8 teaspoon)
Onion, chopped (2 teaspoons)

Directions:
1. Place avocado in a small mixing bowl. Add hot sauce, sour cream, and onion. Stir well to combine.
2. Serve along with sliced veggies or baked tortilla chips.
3. Enjoy.

Serving size = 1/4 cup

Servings: 4

Nutrition Information: 8 g total carbohydrate, 2 g dietary fiber, 51 mg sodium, 1 g saturated fat, 5 g total fat, 0 g trans fat, 3 mg cholesterol, 2 g protein, 3 g monounsaturated fat, 85 calories, 0 g added sugars.

Pesto-Filled Mushrooms

Ingredients:
Mushrooms, crimini, washed, w/ stems removed (20 pieces)
Filling:
Pumpkin seeds (2 tablespoons)
Lemon juice (2 teaspoons)
Basil leaves, fresh (2 cups)
Cheese, Parmesan, fresh (1/4 cup)
Garlic, fresh, minced (1 tablespoon)
Olive oil, extra-virgin (1 tablespoon)
Salt, kosher (1/2 teaspoon)
Topping:
Butter, melted (1/4 cup)
Breadcrumbs, panko (1 ½ cups)
Parsley, fresh, chopped (3 tablespoons)

Directions:
1. Set the oven to 350 degrees to preheat. Meanwhile, place the mushroom caps on a large baking sheet (face-down).
2. Pour the panko breadcrumbs into a small bowl. Add the parsley and butter, then stir well to combine. Set aside while you prepare the filling.
3. Place in a blender the following: cheese, oil, lemon juice, basil, salt, garlic, and pumpkin seeds. Process until the ingredients is combined.
4. Fill each mushroom cap with the prepared filling. After sprinkling the mushrooms with panko (1 teaspoon each) on top, gently pat down and place in the oven to bake for about ten to fifteen minutes or until they turn golden brown.

Serving size = 1 mushroom
Servings: 20

Nutrition Information: 4 g total carbohydrate, 0 g dietary fiber, 80 mg sodium, 2 g saturated fat, 3 g total fat, 0 g trans fat, 7 mg cholesterol, 2 g protein, 1 g monounsaturated fat, 59 calories, 0 g total sugars.

Sweet Coconut Shrimp

Ingredients:
Breadcrumbs, panko (1/4 cup)
Shrimp, large, peeled, deveined (12 pieces)
Coconut, sweetened (1/4 cups)
Salt, kosher (1/2 teaspoon)
Coconut milk (1/2 cup)

Directions:
1. Set the oven to 375 degrees to preheat. Meanwhile, use cooking spray to lightly coat a large baking sheet.
2. Place the panko breadcrumbs in the food processor. Add the coconut and salt, then process until you have an evenly smooth mixture. Transfer into a small bowl. Meanwhile, pour the coconut milk in a separate bowl.
3. Dip the shrimps in the coconut milk before dipping in the panko mixture as well. Place the coated shrimps on the prepped baking sheet before lightly coating with cooking spray on top.
4. Place the shrimps in the oven to bake for ten to fifteen minutes or until golden brown.

Serving size = 2 shrimps
Servings: 6
Nutrition Information: 4 g total carbohydrate, 0 g dietary fiber, 396 g sodium, 2 g saturated fat, 4 g total fat, 0 g trans fat, 48 mg cholesterol, 5 g protein, 2 g monounsaturated fat, 75 calories, 2 g total sugars.

Gingery Grilled Portobello

Ingredients:
Pineapple juice (1/2 cup)
Mushrooms, portobello, large (4 pieces)
Basil, fresh, chopped (1 tablespoon)
Vinegar, balsamic (1/4 cup)
Ginger, fresh, peeled, chopped (2 tablespoons)

Directions:
1. Use a damp cloth to clean the mushrooms before removing their stems. Arrange in a large glass dish with their stem-less sides up. Set aside.
2. Pour the pineapple juice and vinegar in a small mixing bowl. Add the ginger and stir well to combine.
3. Top the mushrooms with a drizzling of the prepared marinade. Cover before placing in the refrigerator to marinate for one hour, making sure to turn the mushrooms halfway.
4. Heat a broiler/gas grill/charcoal grill. Use cooking spray to coat the broiler pan/grill rack. Make sure to place the cooking rack four to six inches from the source of heat.
5. Broil/grill the mushrooms on medium for five minutes on every side or until tender, turning often as you go. Keep the mushrooms from drying out by basting with the marinade.
6. Use tongs to transfer the mushrooms onto a serving platter. Top with basil and serve right away.

Serving size = 1 mushroom
Servings: 4
Nutrition Information: 13 g total carbohydrate, 2 g dietary fiber, 15 mg sodium, trace saturated fat, trace total fat, 0 g trans fat, 0 mg cholesterol, 3 g protein, trace monounsaturated fat, 65 calories, 0 g added sugars.

Yummy Peanut Butter Hummus

Ingredients:
Sugar, brown (2 tablespoons)
Beans, garbanzo (2 cups)
Peanut butter, powdered (1/2 cup)
Peanut butter, natural (1/4 cup)
Vanilla extract (1 teaspoon)
Water (1 cup)

Directions:
1. Pour the water in a food processor. Add the brown sugar, peanut butter, garbanzo beans and vanilla extract.
2. Process until the mixture is smooth.
3. Place in the refrigerator for up to a week.

Serving size = 2 tablespoons
Servings: 16
Nutrition Information: 19 g total carbohydrate, 4 g dietary fiber, 47 mg sodium, 0 g saturated fat, 4 g total fat, 0 g trans fat, 0 mg cholesterol, 7 g protein, 1 g monounsaturated fat, 135 calories, 4 g total sugars.

BREADS

Apricot-Almond Biscotti

Ingredients:
Milk, one-percent low-fat (2 tablespoons)
Flour, plain/all-purpose (3/4 cup)
Almond extract (1/2 teaspoon)
Baking powder (1 teaspoon)
Apricots, dried, chopped (2/3 cup)
Sugar, brown, firmly packed (1/4 cup)
Honey, dark (2 tablespoons)
Flour, whole meal/whole wheat (3/4 cup)
Eggs, beaten lightly (2 pieces)
Oil, canola (2 tablespoons)
Almonds, chopped coarsely (1/4 cup)

Directions:
1. Set the oven to 350 degrees to preheat.
2. Place the brown sugar, baking powder, and flours in a large mixing bowl. Whisk until the ingredients are combined before adding in the honey, milk, almond extract, canola oil, and eggs. Use a wooden spoon to stir until the mixture turns into dough.
3. Stir in the chopped almonds and apricots, then blend some more with your floured hands.
4. Transfer the dough onto a long plastic wrap sheet. Mold the dough to form a flattened log that measures twelve inches long, three inches wide, and one inch high. Raise the wrap to invert the flattened dough onto a baking sheet (nonstick).
5. Place in the oven to bake for about twenty-five to thirty minutes or until lightly browned. Let sit on another baking sheet for about ten minutes or until cooled while leaving the oven set to 350 degrees.

6. Transfer the cooled dough onto a cutting board. Use a serrated knife to slice it diagonally into 24 half-inch-wide crosswise sections. Place the dough slices on a baking sheet with their cut sides down.

7. Place in the oven to bake for about fifteen to twenty minutes or until crisp. When done, place on a wire rack and let stand to cool.

8. Store the cookies in an airtight jar.

Serving size = 1 cookie
Servings: 24 cookies
Nutrition Information: 11 g total carbohydrate, 1 g dietary fiber, 20 mg sodium, trace saturated fat, 2 g total fat, 0 g trans fat, 15 mg cholesterol, 2 g protein, 1 g monounsaturated fat, 70 calories, 3 g added sugars.

Corn Apple Muffins

Ingredients:
Cornmeal, yellow (1/2 cup)
Apple, peeled, chopped coarsely (1 piece)
Baking powder (1 tablespoon)
Egg whites (2 pieces)
Sugar, brown, packed (1/4 cup)
Corn kernels (1/2 cup)
Flour, all-purpose (2 cups)
Salt (1/4 teaspoon)
Milk, fat-free (3/4 cup)

Directions:
1. Set the oven to 425 degrees to preheat. Meanwhile, use foil or paper liners to line a muffin tin (twelve-cup capacity).
2. Place the flour, brown sugar, salt, cornmeal, and baking powder in a large mixing bowl. Stir well to combine.
3. In another bowl, whisk the egg whites and milk together. Add the corn kernels and chopped apple and whisk until evenly combined. Pour the mixture over the dry ingredients and then stir gently, making sure the flour mixture becomes slightly moist and lumpy.
4. Pour the batter into the muffin cups (about two-thirds full). Place in the oven to bake for half an hour or until the surface of the muffins are springy to the touch.
5. Serve and enjoy.

Serving size = 1 muffin
Servings: 12 muffins
Nutrition Information: 26 g total carbohydrate, 1 g dietary fiber, 127 mg sodium, trace saturated fat, < 1 g total fat, 0 g trans fat, trace cholesterol, 4 g protein,

trace monounsaturated fat, 120 calories, 3 g added sugars.

Quick and Spicy Carrot Bread

Ingredients:

Sugar, brown, firmly packed (1/4 cup + 2 tablespoons)
Flour, whole wheat (1 cup)
Egg whites (2 pieces) or egg substitute, beaten (equivalent to one egg)
Cinnamon, ground (1/2 teaspoon)
Carrots, shredded (1 ½ cups)
Baking soda (1/2 teaspoon)
Vanilla extract (1 teaspoon)
Margarine, trans fat-free, warmed to room temp. (1/3 cup)
Raisins, golden (2 tablespoons)
Flour, all-purpose, sifted (1/2 cup)
Ginger, ground (1/4 teaspoon)
Milk, skim (1/3 cup)
Orange juice, unsweetened (2 tablespoons)
Walnuts, chopped finely (1 tablespoon)
Baking powder (2 teaspoons)
Orange rind, grated (1 teaspoon)

Directions:

1. Set the oven to 375 degrees to preheat. Meanwhile, use cooking spray to coat a loaf pan (2 ½" x 8 ½" x 4 ½").
2. In a small mixing bowl, stir together the whole wheat flour, all-purpose flour, skim milk, baking soda, baking powder, and ground cinnamon. Let it sit.
3. In another bowl, whisk together the sugar and margarine until creamy. Whisk in the egg, milk, orange rind, orange juice, and vanilla.
4. Stir in the raisins, shredded carrots, and chopped walnuts before adding in the reserved dry mixture.
5. Transfer the batter onto the prepped loaf pan. Place in the oven to bake for about forty-five minutes.

6. Let stand to cool for about ten minutes.
7. Take out of the pan and allow to completely cool on a wire rack.
8. Serve and enjoy.

Serving size = 1/2–inch slice
Servings: 17
Nutrition Information: 15 g total carbohydrate, 1 g dietary fiber, 82 mg sodium, 1 g saturated fat, 5 g total fat, 0 g trans fat, trace cholesterol, 2 g protein, 2 g monounsaturated fat, 110 calories, 6 g added sugars.

Delicious Breakfast Bars

Ingredients:
Almonds, flaked (1/2 cup) or pecans, toasted, chopped (1/2 cup)
Milk, dry, fat-free (1/2 cup)
Peanut butter, natural, unsalted (1/2 cup)
Flour, soy (1/2 cup)
Salt (1/2 teaspoon)
Oats, old-fashioned, rolled (2 ½ cups)
Olive oil (1 tablespoon)
Wheat germ, toasted (1/2 cup)
Apples, dried, chopped (1/2 cup)
Raisins (1/2 cup)
Vanilla extract (2 teaspoons)
Honey, dark (2 teaspoons)

Directions:
1. Set the oven to 325 degrees to preheat. Meanwhile, use cooking spray (olive oil) to coat a baking pan (9" x 13").
2. Place the flour, wheat germ, apples, salt, oats, dry milk, almonds and raisin in a large mixing bowl. Stir well to combine. Set aside.
3. Heat a small saucepan on medium-low before adding the olive oil, honey, and peanut butter, Stir well to combine before adding the vanilla. Make sure the mixture does not boil.
4. Pour the honey mixture into the dry mixture and quickly blend. The resulting mixture should be just a bit sticky.
5. Transfer the mixture onto the prepped baking pan and pat evenly. Remove air pockets by pressing firmly and then place in the oven to bake for twenty-five minutes or until the edges are lightly browned.
6. Let sit on the pan (set on the wire rack) for about ten minutes before cutting into bars (24 pieces).

7. Take the bars out of the pan and allow to completely cool on the wire rack before placing in an airtight jar.
8. Store in the refrigerator.

Serving size = 1 bar
Servings: 24 bars
Nutrition Information: 27 g total carbohydrate, 3 g dietary fiber, 75m g sodium, 1 g saturated fat, 5 g total fat, 0 g trans fat, 1 mg cholesterol, 6 g protein, 2 g monounsaturated fat, 177 calories, 11 g added sugars.

Mouthwatering Zucchini Bread

Ingredients:
Flour, whole meal/whole wheat (1 ¼ cups)
Applesauce, unsweetened (1/2 cup)
Cinnamon, ground (3 teaspoons)
Oil, canola (1/4 cup)
Pineapple, unsweetened, crushed (1 ½ cups)
Vanilla extract (2 teaspoons)
Baking soda (1 teaspoon)
Zucchini, shredded (2 cups)
Egg whites (6 pieces)
Flour, all-purpose/plain (1 ¼ cups)
Baking powder (1 teaspoon)
Walnuts, chopped (1/2 cup)
Sugar (1/2 cup)

Directions:
1. Set the oven to 350 degrees to preheat. Use cooking spray to lightly coat two loaf pans (9" x 5").
2. Place the egg whites, apple sauce, vanilla, canola oil, and vanilla in a large mixing bowl. Beat on low speed with an electric mixer until the mixture is foamy and thick.
3. In another bowl, combine the flours and then set aside ½ cup of the flour mixture. Stir in the cinnamon, baking soda, and baking powder.
4. Combine the egg white mixture and flour mixture on medium speed with an electric mixer. Stir in the pineapple, walnuts and zucchini. Add the rest of the flour mixture to adjust the batter's consistency (it should be thick instead of runny).
5. Fill each prepped pan with one-half of the batter. Place in the oven to bake for about fifty minutes.
6. Allow the bread to cool for ten minutes in the pans (placed on the wire rack). Invert the loaves and allow to completely cool on the rack.

7. Slice the loaves into one-inch slices (9 pieces).
8. Serve and enjoy.

Serving size = 1 slice
Servings: 18 slices
Nutrition Information: 22 g total carbohydrate, 2 g dietary fiber, 103 mg sodium, 0.5 g saturated fat, 5 g total fat, 0 g trans fat, 0 mg cholesterol, 4 g protein, 2 g monounsaturated fat, 141 calories, 5 g added sugars.

Chapter 3 – Guaranteed Low-Sodium Breakfast, Dessert and Beverage Recipes

Complement your DASH Diet with regular physical activity. This will help give your efforts to lower blood pressure and lose weight (such as following the recipes provided in this book) a boost.

BREAKFAST

Hot Pearl Barley Cereal

Ingredients:
Oats, steel-cut, uncooked (1/4 cup)
Wheat berries, red, uncooked (1/2 cup)
Salt, kosher (1/2 teaspoon)
Pearl barley, uncooked (1/2 cup)
Rice, brown, uncooked (1/2 cup)
Quinoa, uncooked (3 tablespoons)
Water (1 ½ quarts)

Directions:
1. Fill a large saucepan with the wheat berries, oats, barley, rice and quinoa. Add the salt and water, then heat on medium. Stir and allow the mixture to boil before reducing heat to low. Let the mixture simmer for about forty-five minutes, making sure to stir occasionally.

Serving size = ½ cup
Servings: 14
Nutrition Information: 21 g total carbohydrate, 3 g dietary fiber, 74 mg sodium, 0 g saturated fat, 1 g total fat, 0 g trans fat, 0 mg cholesterol, 4 g protein, 0 g monounsaturated fat, 114 calories, 0 total sugars.

Simply Delicious Baked Oatmeal

Ingredients:
Oats, rolled, uncooked (3 cups)
Applesauce, unsweetened (1/2 cup)
Cinnamon (1 teaspoon)
Sugar, brown (1/3 cup)
Oil, canola (1 tablespoon)
Egg whites (4 pieces) or egg substitute = 2 eggs
Milk, skim (1 cup)
Baking powder (2 teaspoons)

Directions:
1. Pour the applesauce into a large mixing bowl. Add eggs, sugar and oil. Stir well to combine.
2. Stir in the oats, brown sugar, cinnamon, baking powder and skim milk. Meanwhile, use cooking spray to generously coat a baking pan (9x13).
3. Transfer the oatmeal mixture into the baking pan. Place in the oven to bake for about thirty minutes, uncovered.
4. Serve immediately.

Serving size = ¾ cup
Servings: 8
Nutrition Information: 33 g total carbohydrate, 3 g dietary fiber, 105 mg sodium, 0.5 g saturated fat, 4 g total fat, 0 g trans fat, 0.5 mg cholesterol, 7 g protein, 2 g monounsaturated fat, 196 calories, 8.5 g added sugars.

Buckwheat and Strawberry Pancakes

Ingredients:
Flour, buckwheat (1/2 cup)
Milk, fat-free (1/2 cup)
Water, sparkling (1/2 cup)
Sugar (1 tablespoon)
Egg whites (2 pieces)
Flour, all-purpose/plain (1/2 cup)
Baking powder (1 tablespoon)
Strawberries, fresh, sliced (3 cups)
Oil, canola (1 tablespoon)

Directions:
1. Combine the milk, egg whites and canola oil in a small mixing bowl.
2. In a separate bowl, whisk the sugar, baking powder and flours together. Stir in the prepared egg white mixture along with the sparkling water, making sure the entire mixture becomes slightly moistened.
3. Heat on medium a griddle or frying pan (nonstick). Add pancake batter (1/2 cup) and cook for two minutes or until the pancake has bubbles n the surface and its edges are a bit brown. Flip and cook for another two minutes or until the pancake is done and well-browned. Do the same with the rest of the pancake batter.
4. Serve pancakes on individual plates, topping each with sliced strawberries (1/2 cup).
5. Enjoy.

Serving size = 1 pancake
Servings: 6
Nutrition Information: 24 g total carbohydrate, 3 g dietary fiber, 150 mg sodium, trace saturated fat, 3 g total fat, 0 g trans fat, trace cholesterol, 5 g protein, 2 g monounsaturated fat, 143 calories.

Cinnamon Toast

Ingredients:
Cinnamon bread (4 slices)
Egg whites (4 pieces)
Nutmeg, ground (1/8 teaspoon)
Cinnamon, ground (1/4 teaspoon)
Vanilla (1 teaspoon)
Maple syrup (1/4 cup)

Directions:
1. Place the egg whites in a small mixing bowl. Add nutmeg and vanilla, then stir well to combine.
2. Dip the cinnamon bread sliced into the prepared egg mixture, making sure all sides are evenly coated.
3. Meanwhile, heat a griddle or frying pan (nonstick) on medium. Once heated, add the egg mixture-coated bread.
4. Sprinkle the bread with cinnamon and then allow to cook for about four to five minutes per side or until golden brown.
5. Transfer the French toast onto warmed plates (2 slices/plate). Top with powdered sugar (1 teaspoon/plate) and maple syrup (2 tablespoon/plate).
6. Serve right away and enjoy.

Serving size = 2 slices
Servings: 2
Nutrition Information: < 1 g dietary fiber, 334 mg sodium, trace saturated fat, 3 g total fat, 0 g trans fat, 0 mg cholesterol, 11 g protein, trace monounsaturated fat, 299 calories, 17 g added sugars.

Chilled Oatmeal

Ingredients:
Yogurt, Greek, low-fat (1/4 cup)
Chia seeds, dried (1 ½ teaspoons)
Milk, skim/soy (1/3 cup)
Oats, rolled, old-fashioned (1/4 cup)
Apples, diced (1/4 cup)
Cinnamon (1/4 teaspoon)
Applesauce, unsweetened (1/4 cup)

Directions:
1. Fill a mason jar (1-pint) with the Greek yogurt, applesauce, and skim/soy milk. Mix well.
2. Add the chia seeds, rolled oats, cinnamon, and diced apples. Stir well to combine.
3. Cover and shake until all ingredients are well-combined.
4. Place in the refrigerator overnight.
5. Serve chilled.

Serving size = 1 cup
Servings: 1
Nutrition Information: 30 g total carbohydrate, 6 g dietary fiber, 89 mg sodium, 0 g saturated fat, 4 g total fat, 0 g trans fat, 4 mg cholesterol, 11 g protein, 1 g monounsaturated fat, 193 calories, 17 g added sugars.

DESSERT

Blueberry and Apple Cobbler

Ingredients:
Lemon juice (1 tablespoon)
Cinnamon, ground (1 teaspoon)
Cornstarch (2 tablespoons)
Blueberries, fresh/frozen (12 ounces)
Apples, large, peeled, cored, sliced thinly (2 pieces)
Sugar (2 tablespoons)
Topping:
Margarine, trans-free, cold, sliced into one-inch cuts (4 tablespoons)
Sugar (2 tablespoons)
Milk, fat-free (1/2 cup)
Flour, all-purpose (3/4 cup)
Baking powder (1 ½ teaspoons)
Salt (1/4 teaspoon)
Vanilla extract (1 teaspoon)
Flour, whole wheat (3/4 cup)

Directions:
1. Set the oven to 400 degrees to preheat. Meanwhile, use cooking spray to lightly coat a baking dish (9-inch).
2. Place the apple slices in a large mixing bowl. Sprinkle lemon juice on top and set aside.
3. In a separate bowl, mix the cornstarch, sugar, and cinnamon together. Gently toss the mixture with the apples before stirring in the blueberries.
4. Transfer the blueberry-apple mixture onto the prepped baking dish and spread to form an even layer. Let stand.
5. In another large mixing bowl, mix the sugar, flour, salt and baking powder together. Cut the margarine

into the flour mixture with a fork, making sure the mixture transforms into coarse crumbs.

6. Pour in the milk and vanilla, then stir until the mixture becomes a moist dough. Transfer the dough onto a work surface generously sprinkled with flour.

7. Use floured hands to gently knead the dough about six to eight times to make it smooth and easier to mold.

8. Roll dough into half-inch-thick rectangles with a rolling pin. Cut out your desired shapes with a cookie cutter,

9. Place the cut dough pieces on top of the blueberry-apple mixture. Place in the oven to bake for about half an hour.

10. Serve warm.

Serving size = 1/8 portion of recipe
Servings: 8
Nutrition Information: 38 g total carbohydrate, 4 g dietary fiber, 202 mg sodium, 1 g saturated fat, 6 g total fat, 0 g trans fat, trace cholesterol, 4 g protein, 2 g monounsaturated fat, 222 calories, 6 g added sugars.

Decadent Fruit Dessert

Ingredients:
Oranges, mandarin, drained (11 ounces)
Yogurt, fat-free, plain (1/2 cup)
Cream cheese, fat-free, softened (4 ounces)
Vanilla (1/2 teaspoon)
Peaches, water-packed, drained, sliced (8.25 ounces)
Coconut, shredded, toasted (4 tablespoons)
Pineapple chunks, water-packed, drained (8 ounces)
Sugar (1 teaspoon)

Directions:
1. Place the cream cheese in a small mixing bowl. Add the yogurt, vanilla and sugar and beat on high speed with an electric mixer until the mixture is smooth.
2. In another bowl, mix together the pineapple, oranges and peaches. Fold the cream cheese mixture into the fruit mixture.
3. Cover and place in the refrigerator to chill for about eight hours.
4. Transfer the prepared fruit dessert into a serving bowl or in four small bowls. Serve topped with shredded coconut.
5. Enjoy.

Serving size = 1 slice
Servings: 12
Nutrition Information: 24 g total carbohydrate, 3 g dietary fiber, 168 mg sodium, 4 g saturated fat, 6 g total fat, trace trans fat, 6 mg cholesterol, 4 g protein, 0.5 g monounsaturated fat, 150 calories, 13 g added sugars.

Heavenly Chocolate Cake

Ingredients:
Yam, roasted, mashed (2 tablespoons)
Salt, kosher (1/4 teaspoon)
Applesauce, unsweetened (1/4 cup)
Baking soda (1 teaspoon)
Yogurt, Greek, plain, fat-free (1/2 cup)
Chocolate, dark, unsweetened (2 ounces)
Pastry flour, whole wheat (1 ½ cups)
Water (2 tablespoons)
Butter, unsalted, softened (2 tablespoons)
Sugar, brown, lightly packed (1/4 cup)
Vanilla (1 ½ teaspoons)
Water, boiling (1/2 cup)
Honey (1/4 cup)
Chia seeds (2 teaspoons)
For topping:
Strawberries, thinly sliced (12 ounces)
Dark chocolate bar, melted (2 ounces)
Cinnamon (2 teaspoons)

Directions:
1. Set the oven to 375 degrees to preheat. Meanwhile, use cooking spray to coat a round cake pan (9-inch) before lightly dusting with flour.
2. Sift together the flour, salt and baking soda into a large mixing bowl. Let stand.
3. In another bowl, combine the water and chia seeds, then allow to gel by setting aside.
4. Gradually melt the chocolate, then let it cool a bit (make sure it is not allowed to harden).
5. In a large mixing bowl, mix the applesauce, yams, honey and brown sugar. Beat for about two minutes before adding the chia gel. Beat for another two minutes, then add the chocolate and vanilla. Beat for a minute before gradually stirring in the yogurt (1/2

portion) and flour mixture (1/2 portion). Do the same with the remaining yogurt and flour mixture.

6. Gradually add the boiling water to the flour-yogurt mixture, stirring as you go. Transfer the batter into the prepped cake pan. Place in the oven to bake for twenty minutes or until moist but not gooey.

7. Remove from the oven and let cool on a wire rack for twenty minutes. After taking the cake out of the pan, slice into 12 pieces and drizzle melted chocolate bar on top.

8. Place cake slices on individual plates and serve garnished with cinnamon and strawberries.

Serving size = 1 slice
Servings: 12
Nutrition Information: 24 g total carbohydrate, 3 g dietary fiber, 168 mg sodium, 4 g saturated fat, 6 g total fat, trace trans fat, 6 mg cholesterol, 4 g protein, 0.5 g monounsaturated fat, 150 calories, 13 g added sugars.

Divine Lemon Cheesecake

Ingredients:
Sugar (1/4 cup)
Lemon juice (2 tablespoons)
Cottage cheese, low-fat (2 cups)
Vanilla (1 teaspoon)
Water, cold (2 tablespoons)
Milk, skim, almost boiling (1/2 cup)
Egg whites (2 pieces) or egg substitute = 1 egg
Lemon zest (1/2 teaspoon)
Gelatin, unflavored (1 envelope)

Directions:
1. Pour water in the blender. Add the lemon juice and gelatin and stir well to combine. Process for one to two minutes on low speed to ensure the gelatin is softened.
2. Pour in the hot milk and stir well to dissolve the gelatin. Add the cheese, sugar, vanilla and egg substitute. Stir well to combine. Process for one to two minutes or until the mixture is evenly smooth.
3. Transfer the mixture onto a flat, round dish or a pie plate (9-inch). Place in the refrigerator to chill for two to three hours.
4. Serve topped with lemon zest (grated) and enjoy.

Serving size = 1/8 portion of cake
Servings: 8
Nutrition Information: 9 g total carbohydrate, trace dietary fiber, 252 mg sodium, trace saturated fat, 1 g total fat, 0 g trans fat, 3 mg cholesterol, 9 g protein, trace monounsaturated fat, 80 calories, 9 g added sugars.

Squash and Sweet Potato Pie

Ingredients:
Flour, rye (1/4 cup)
Tofu, silken (1 teaspoon)
Orange zest (1 teaspoon)
Butternut squash, peeled, seeded, cooked (2 ½ pounds)
Ginger, fresh, grated (1 teaspoon)
Honey (3 tablespoons)
Sweet potato, peeled, cooked (1/4 pound)
Egg whites (1/4 cup)
Clove (1/2 teaspoon)
Nutmeg (1/2 teaspoon)
Cinnamon (1/2 teaspoon)
Vanilla extract (1/2 teaspoon)
Pie shell, pre-made, 9-inch, frozen (1 piece)
Milk, soy (1/2 cup)

Directions:
1. Set the oven to 300 degrees to preheat.
2. Place the butternut squash and sweet potato in a food processor. Puree and transfer into a large mixing bowl.
3. Add the rye flour, silken tofu, orange zest, grated ginger, honey, egg whites, soy milk, clove, nutmeg, cinnamon, and vanilla extract. Stir until mixture is well-combined and smooth.
4. Set the pie shell on the sheet pan. Fill the pie shell with the squash and sweet potato mixture. Place in the oven to bake for about forty-five to fifty-five minutes or until an internal temperature of 180 degrees is reached.
5. Serve and enjoy.

Serving size = 1/8 portion of pie
Servings: 8

Nutrition Information: 34 g total carbohydrate, 4 g dietary fiber, 109 mg sodium, 2 g saturated fat, 6 g total fat, 0 g trans fat, 0 mg cholesterol, 5 g protein, 3 g monounsaturated fat, 210 calories, 7 g added sugars.

BEVERAGE

Blueberry-Lavender Lemonade

Ingredients:
Blueberries (16 ounces)
Lavender flowers, dried (1 tablespoon)
Lemon juice (1 cup)
Sugar, granulated (1/4 cup)
Water, cold (2 cups + 1/4 cup)
Sweetener, Splenda (2 tablespoons)
Ice cubes (4 cups)

Directions:
1. Fill a pitcher (1-gallon) with ice cubes. Set aside.
2. Fill a medium saucepan with cold water (2 cups) and bring to a boil.
3. Stir in the sugar, lavender, and blueberries. Allow the mixture to boil for five minutes or until the sugar is well-dissolved and the blueberries have burst.
4. Pour the blueberry mixture onto a strainer set over the ice-filled pitcher.
5. Stir in the lemon juice, cold water (1/4 cup).
6. Serve right away.

Serving size = 8 ounces
Servings: 16
Nutrition Information: 8 g total carbohydrate, 0 g dietary fiber, 7 mg sodium, 0 g saturated fat, 0 g trans fat, 0 mg cholesterol, 0 g protein, 0 g monounsaturated fat, 33 calories, 7 g total sugars.

Lime and Mint Iced Tea

Ingredients:
Lime juice concentrate (2 tablespoons)
Tea, unsweetened, freshly brewed, cooled (1 cup)
Mint leaves, fresh (2 tablespoons + 1 sprig)
Sugar substitute (1/2 teaspoon)
Ice cubes (5 to 6 pieces)

Directions:
1. Pour the lime juice and tea into a blender.
2. Add the ice cubes and mint leaves, then stir well.
3. Process until well-blended, smooth and frothy.
4. Serve in a chilled glass and top with a sprig of mint.

Serving size = 1 glass
Servings: 1
Nutrition Information: 4 g total carbohydrate, 0 g dietary fiber, 9 mg sodium, 0 g saturated fat, 0 g total fat, 0 g trans fat, 0 mg cholesterol, 0 g protein, 0 g monounsaturated fat, 16 calories.

Cranberry Punch

Ingredients:
Citrus fruit, peeled (2 cups)
Pineapple, chopped (1 ½ cups)
Lemon juice (1 piece)
Ice cubes (1 cup + 2 pieces)
Cranberry juice (8 ounces)

Directions:
1. Pour the cranberry juice and lemon juice in a blender. Stir well before adding the citrus fruit and chopped pineapple.
2. Process until extremely smooth in texture before adding the ice.
3. Process again and pour into a tall glass.
4. Serve and enjoy.

Serving size = ¾ cup
Servings: 6
Nutrition Information: 18 g total carbohydrate, 2 g dietary fiber, 2 mg sodium, 0 g saturated fat, trace total fat, 0 g trans fat, 0 mg cholesterol, 1 g protein, 0 g monounsaturated fat, 76 calories, 0 g added sugars.

Iced Almond Latte

Ingredients:
Milk, fat-free (1 ½ cups)
Coffee, espresso, decaffeinated, brewed, cooled (2 cups)
Almond syrup, sugar-free (2 tablespoons)
Ice cubes (1 cup)
Espresso beans, ground (1 teaspoon)
Topping, fat-free, whipped (1 cup)
Brown sugar, golden (2 tablespoons)

Directions:
1. Mix together the milk, espresso, syrup and brown sugar in a pitcher.
2. Place in the refrigerator for two hours or until well-chilled.
3. Meanwhile, place the ice cubes in 4 glasses. Fill each glass with the chilled coffee and whipped topping (1/4 cup).
4. Top with the ground espresso beans and serve immediately.

Serving size = 1 glass (8 fl. oz.)
Servings: 4
Nutrition Information: 11 g total carbohydrate, 0 g dietary fiber, 69 mg sodium, 1 g saturated fat, 0 g total fat, 3 mg cholesterol, 4 g protein, trace monounsaturated fat, 70 calories, 7 g added sugars.

Banana and Strawberry Milkshake

Ingredients:
Milk, soy (1/2 cup)
Strawberries, frozen, chopped (6 pieces)
Banana, medium (1 piece)
Strawberries, fresh, sliced (2 pieces)
Yogurt, vanilla, fat-free, frozen (1 cup)

Directions:
1. Fill a blender with the frozen yogurt and strawberries.
2. Stir in the soy milk and process until well-blended and smooth.
3. Fill 2 tall frosty glasses with the puree. Top with the fresh strawberry slices.
4. Serve right away.

Serving size = 1 cup
Servings: 2
Nutrition Information: 40 g total carbohydrate, 8 g dietary fiber, 117 mg sodium, trace saturated fat, 1 g total fat, 0 g trans fat, 0 mg cholesterol, 6 g protein, 0 g monounsaturated fat, 183 calories, 17 g added sugars.

Chapter 4 – Blood Pressure-Lowering Fish, Chicken and Pasta Recipes

Following the DASH Diet is no easy feat, which is why it is important that you forgive yourself if you slip up sometimes. It is equally important that you reward yourself for your efforts and accomplishments – just make sure your rewards are of the non-treat kind). You could buy a book, rent a DVD, go out with a friend, or experiment with more DASH Diet recipes!

MAIN DISH - FISH

Asian-Flavored Baked Salmon
Ingredients:
Garlic, minced (2 cloves)
Sesame oil (1/4 teaspoon)
Soy sauce, low-sodium (1 teaspoon)
Black pepper, ground (1/2 teaspoon)
Pineapple juice, w/out added sugar (1/2 cup)
Ginger, ground (1/4 teaspoon)
Fillets, salmon, four-ounce (2 pieces)
Mango/papaya/pineapple, fresh, diced (1 cup)

Directions:
1. Pour the pineapple juice in a small mixing bowl. Add the soy sauce, garlic, and ginger. Stir well to combine.
2. Place the salmon fillets inside a baking dish (small) and arrange to form a single layer. Fill the dish with the prepared pineapple juice mixture, making sure the fillets are evenly covered.

3. Place in the refrigerator and allow to marinate for about an hour, turning the fillets every fifteen minutes.

4. Set the oven at 375 degrees. Meanwhile, use cooking spray to lightly coat aluminum foil that is cut into two squares.

5. Place 1 marinated fillet inside each foil square. After drizzling with sesame oil (1/8 teaspoon each), top with diced fruit (1/2 cup each) and sprinkle with pepper. Seal the squares by wrapping the foil around each fillet and then folding the edges.

6. Place in the oven to bake for ten minutes per side or until each fillet is opaque all the way through.

7. Place each fillet on a warmed plate. Serve and enjoy.

Serving size = 1 fillet
Servings: 2
Nutrition Information: 19 g total carbohydrate, 2 g dietary fiber, 192 mg sodium, 1 g saturated fat, 7 g total fat, trace trans fat, 57 mg cholesterol, 27 g protein, 3 g monounsaturated fat, 247 calories, 0g added sugars.

Broiled Bass

Ingredients:
Lemon juice (1 tablespoon)
Fillets, white sea bass, four-ounce (2 pieces)
Garlic, minced (1 teaspoon)
Black pepper, ground (1/2 teaspoon)
Herb seasoning blend, salt-free (1/4 teaspoon)

Directions:
1. Heat the grill (broiler), making sure the rack is positioned four inches away from the source of heat.
2. Meanwhile, use cooking spray to lightly coat a baking pan before place the fillets inside.
3. Top each fillet with lemon juice, herbed seasoning, garlic and pepper. Place in the broiler to cook for about eight to ten minutes or until the fillets are opaque.
4. Serve right away.

Serving size = 1 fillet
Servings: 2
Nutrition Information: < 1 g total carbohydrate, 10 mg dietary fiber, 77 mg sodium, 1 g saturated fat, 2 g total fat, 0 g trans fat, 46 mg cholesterol, 21 g protein, < 1 g monounsaturated fat, 102 calories, 0 g added sugars.

Maple Salmon Roast

Ingredients:
Fillets, salmon, sliced into 6 pieces (2 pounds)
Black pepper, freshly cracked (1/8 teaspoon)
Maple syrup (1/4 cup)
Vinegar, balsamic (1/4 cup)
Salt, kosher (1/4 teaspoon)
Garlic clove, minced (1 piece)
Parsley/mint, fresh (a handful)

Directions:
1. Set the oven to 450 degrees to preheat. Meanwhile, use cooking spray to lightly coat the baking pan.
2. Heat a small saucepan on low before adding the balsamic vinegar, maple syrup and garlic. Allow the mixture to get hot and then remove from the stove.
3. Set aside ½ of the maple syrup mixture for basting; reserve the other half for later.
4. After patting dry the salmon, place on the prepped baking pan with its skin-side down. Brush the prepared maple syrup mixture on top of the salmon before placing in the oven to bake for ten minutes.
5. Baste the salmon again with the maple syrup mixture. Bake for another 5 minutes. Repeat for 3 to 4 times or until the salmon easily flakes.
6. Serve the salmon on individual plates. Top with black pepper, salt, maple syrup mixture (reserved), and parsley/mint.
7. Enjoy.

Serving size = 1 fillet
Servings: 6
Nutrition Information: 10 g total carbohydrate, trace dietary fiber, 150 mg sodium, 1.5 g saturated fat, 10 g total fat, 0 g trans fat, 83 mg cholesterol, 30 g

protein, 3 g monounsaturated fat, 250 calories, 9 g added sugars.

MAIN DISH - CHICKEN

Wild Rice and Baked Chicken

Ingredients:
Broth, chicken, unsalted (2 cups)
Pearl onions, whole (1 ½ cups)
Celery, chopped finely (1 ½ cups)
Tarragon, fresh (1 teaspoon)
Rice, long grain, uncooked (3/4 cups)
Wine, white, dry (1 ½ cups)
Rice, wild, uncooked (3/4 cup)
Chicken breast halves, boneless, skinless (1 pound)

Directions:
1. Set the oven to 300 degrees to preheat.
2. Slice chicken breasts into one-inch cuts.
3. Heat a frying pan (nonstick) on medium and add the chicken cuts, pearl onions, celery and tarragon.
4. Pour in the chicken broth (1 cup) and cook for about ten minutes or until the vegetables and chicken are tender. Let sit to cool.
5. Meanwhile, mix together the rest of the chicken broth (1 cup), wine and rice in the baking dish. Allow the mixture to soak for about thirty minutes.
6. Stir in the tender vegetables and chicken before covering. Place in the oven to bake for one hour, making sure the rice does not dry out.
7. Serve right away.

Serving size = 2 cups
Servings: 6
Nutrition Information: 37 g total carbohydrate, 180 mg sodium, 2 g dietary fiber, 3 g total fat, 73 mg cholesterol, 1 g monounsaturated fat, 1 g saturated

fat, 0 g trans fat, 21 g protein, 330 calories, 0 g added sugars.

Balsamic Chicken Roast

Ingredients:
Rosemary, fresh (1 tablespoon) or rosemary, dried (1 teaspoon)
Rosemary, fresh (8 sprigs)
Vinegar, balsamic (1/2 cup)
Chicken, whole, four-pound (1 piece)
Olive oil (1 tablespoon)
Black pepper, freshly ground (1/8 teaspoon)
Sugar, brown (1 teaspoon)
Garlic clove (1 piece)

Directions:
1. Set the oven to 350 degrees.
2. Meanwhile, place the garlic and rosemary in a small mixing bowl. Mince well and set aside.
3. After loosening the chicken flesh from the skin, rub with olive oil plus the garlic-rosemary mixture.
4. Sprinkle the chicken flesh with black pepper before placing two sprigs of rosemary inside its cavity.
5. After trussing the chicken, place in a roasting pan. Cook in the oven got one hour and twenty minutes or until the entire chicken's internal temperature reaches 165 degrees. Make sure to baste the chicken often with the juices in the pan.
6. Transfer the chicken onto a serving platter once it is browned and its juices run clear. Let stand to cool.
7. Pour the balsamic vinegar into a small saucepan. Stir in the brown sugar and then heat on medium for five minutes or until the sugar has completely dissolved. Don't allow the mixture to boil.
8. After carving the chicken, remove the skin and cover with the prepared mixture.
9. Serve topped with the rest of the rosemary sprigs and enjoy right away.

Serving size = 1/8 of chicken
Servings: 8
Nutrition Information: 4 g total carbohydrate, 0 g dietary fiber, 257 mg sodium, 5 g saturated fat, 16 g total fat, 0 g trans fat, 198 mg cholesterol, 51 g protein, 8 g monounsaturated fat, 364 calories, trace added sugars.

Smoky Chicken Quesadillas

Ingredients:
Tomatoes, fresh, chopped (1 cup)
Cheese, cheddar, reduced-fat, shredded (1 cup)
Chicken breasts, skinless, boneless, four-ounce (4 pieces)
Salsa, smoky (1/2 cup)
Cilantro, fresh, chopped (1 cup)
Tortillas, whole wheat, 8-inch diameter (6 pieces)
Onions, chopped (1 cup)

Directions:
1. Set the oven to 425 degrees to preheat. Meanwhile, use cooking spray to lightly coat the cookie sheet.
2. Slice chicken breast into one-inch cubes. Set aside.
3. Heat a large frying pan (nonstick) before adding the onions and cubed chicken. Cook for about five to seven minutes or until the chicken is cooked all the way through and the onions are soft and tender.
4. Take the chicken and onions out of the stove, then add the cilantro, salsa and tomato. Stir well to combine.
5. After laying the tortilla flat, use water to wet the outside edge. Spoon chicken mixture (1/2 cup) on top of the tortilla and spread well, making sure there is a half-inch space between the chicken mixture and the tortilla's outer rim. Add shredded cheese (1 tablespoon) on top before folding the tortilla in half. Seal and then set on the prepped cookie sheet. Do the same with the remaining tortillas.
6. Use cooking spray to lightly coat all tortillas on the surface. Place in the oven to bake for five to seven minutes or until crispy and lightly browned.
7. Slice the baked quesadillas in half before serving immediately.

Serving size = 2 halves
Servings: 6
Nutrition Information: 25 g total carbohydrate, 6 g dietary fiber, 524 mg sodium, 5 g saturated fat, 10 g total fat, trace trans fat, 70 mg cholesterol, 27 g protein, 3 g monounsaturated fat, 298 calories, 0 g added sugars.

MAIN DISH - PASTA

Clams and Corn Fettuccine

Ingredients:
Corn kernels, frozen/fresh (2 cups)
Clams, drained (8 ounces)
Tomatoes, large, seeded, chopped (2 pieces)
Basil, fresh, chopped (4 tablespoons)
Salt (1/4 teaspoon)
Fettuccine, uncooked (10 ounces)
Wine, white (1/2 cup)
Olive oil (1 tablespoon)
Black pepper, ground (1/2 teaspoon)
Garlic, minced (2 tablespoons)

Directions:
1. Pour water into a large pot until it is ¾ full. Allow the water to boil on medium-high before adding the pasta. Cook until al dente while following package directions or for eight minutes.
2. After thoroughly draining the pasta, place in a bowl and set aside.
3. Meanwhile, heat a large saucepan on medium. Add the olive oil, garlic, basil, corn and wine. Stir well to combine and cover. Stirring the mixture frequently, allow to boil before reducing heat to low and adding the pasta along with the clams. Coat the pasta well by tossing gently.
4. Sprinkle pepper and salt.
5. Serve right away.

Serving size = 1 ½ cups
Servings: 6
Nutrition Information: 52 g total carbohydrate, 3 g dietary fiber, 147 mg sodium, 0.5 g saturated fat, 4 g

total fat, trace trans fat, 19 mg cholesterol, 18 g protein, 2 g monounsaturated fat, 316 calories, 0 g added sugars.

Mixed Veggies and Pasta Salad

Ingredients:
Mushrooms, sliced (1 pound)
Olive oil (1 tablespoon)
Bell pepper, green, sliced (1 piece)
Onion, medium, chopped (2 pieces)
Oregano (1/2 teaspoon)
Broth, chicken, low-sodium (1/4 cup)
Zucchini, medium, shredded (2 pieces)
Rotini pasta, whole wheat (12 ounces)
Tomatoes, in juice, unsalted, diced (28 ounces)
Bell pepper, red, sliced (1 piece)
Romaine lettuce (8 leaves)
Garlic, chopped (1 clove)
Basil (1/2 teaspoon)

Directions:
1. Follow package directions in cooking the pasta, then drain thoroughly. Transfer cooked pasta into a serving bowl (large). Set aside after tossing with the olive oil.
2. Heat a large skillet on medium. Pour in the chicken broth. Once broth is heated throughout, stir in the tomatoes, garlic and onions. Cook for five minutes or until the onions are fragrant and transparent.
3. Add the zucchini, red bell pepper, green bell pepper, and mushrooms. Stir well to combine, then add the oregano and basil.
4. Toss the prepared vegetable mixture with the cooked pasta before covering and placing in the refrigerator to chill for an hour.
5. Arrange the lettuce leaves on eight individual plates. Scoop the pasta salad on top.
6. Serve and enjoy.

Serving size = 2 cups

Servings: 8
Nutrition Information: 43 g total carbohydrate, 8 g dietary fiber, 54 mg sodium, 0.5 g saturated fat, 3 g total fat, trace cholesterol, 9 g protein, 1.5 g monounsaturated fat, 235 calories.

Sundried Tomatoes and Rotelle Pasta Salad

Ingredients:
Broth, vegetable, unsalted (1 ¾ cups)
Parsley, fresh, chopped (1/2 cup)
Garlic, mashed (4 cloves)
Olives, black, sliced (1/2 cup)
Rotelle pasta, whole wheat, uncooked (8 ounces)
Cheese, Parmesan (4 teaspoons)
Olive oil (2 tablespoons)
Tomatoes, sundried, dry-packed, water-soaked then drained & chopped (1/3 cup)

Directions:
1. Heat a large skillet on medium before adding the garlic olive oil. Add the sundried tomatoes and stir well.
2. Pour in the vegetable broth and stir again before reducing heat to low. Cover and allow the mixture to simmer for about ten minutes.
3. Pour water into a large pot until it is about ¾ full. Allow the water to boil before adding the rotelle pasta. Cook following package directions until al dente or for about ten to twelve minutes.
4. After draining the pasta thoroughly, toss with the parsley and olives. Once evenly mixed, arrange on four individual plates.
5. Add one-fourth of the tomato mixture to each plate before topping with Parmesan cheese (1 teaspoon).
6. Serve and enjoy.

Serving size = 1 ½ cups
Servings: 4
Nutrition Information: 47 g total carbohydrate, 3 g dietary fiber, 192 mg sodium, 2 g saturated fat, 10 g total fat, 0 g trans fat, 2 mg cholesterol, 10 g protein,

7 g monounsaturated fat, 335 calories, 0 g added sugars.

Vermicelli with Tomato and Asparagus

Ingredients:
Vermicelli, whole grain, dried (4 ounces)
Basil, fresh, chopped (2 tablespoons)
Lemon juice (2 teaspoons)
Cheese, Parmesan, freshly grated (4 tablespoons)
Asparagus (6 spears)
Tomato, medium, chopped (1 piece)
Olive oil (2 teaspoons)
Garlic, minced (1 tablespoon)
Black pepper, ground (1/8 teaspoon)

Directions:
1. Heat a skillet on medium-high before adding olive oil (1 teaspoon).
2. Add the asparagus and sauté for two minutes or until tender-crisp and lightly browned. Take the pan away from the stove and let cool.
3. Slice the cooked asparagus into one-inch cuts and set aside. Meanwhile, pour water into a large pot until about ¾ full. Heat on medium-high. Once the water is boiling, add the pasta and cook for about ten to twelve minutes or until tender (al dente).
4. After draining the pasta thoroughly, place in a large bowl. Add olive oil (1 teaspoon) and toss gently until pasta is evenly coated.
5. Add the cooked asparagus along with the basil, garlic, tomato, and Parmesan cheese (2 tablespoons), then toss again until evenly mixed.
6. Arrange the tossed pasta on individual plates. Top each with Parmesan cheese (1 tablespoon as well as black pepper.
7. Serve right away.

Serving size = 1 cup
Servings: 2

Nutrition Information: 48 g total carbohydrate, 8 g dietary fiber, 158 mg sodium, 2 g saturated fat, 9 g total fat, 9 mg cholesterol, 13 g protein, 4 g monounsaturated fat, 325 calories.

Goat Cheese and Tomato with Penne Pasta

Ingredients:
Cherry tomatoes, halved (1/2 cup)
Black pepper, freshly ground (1/8 teaspoon)
Goat cheese (2 ounces)
Penne pasta, whole wheat (1/3 pound)
Basil, fresh (1/4 cup chopped + 4 whole leaves)
Water (1 tablespoon)
Garlic, minced (1 tablespoon)
Asparagus, chopped into one-inch cuts (1/2 cup)

Directions:
1. Fill a five-gallon pot with water until about ¾ full. Heat on medium-high and allow water to boil before adding the pasta. Cook for about ten to twelve minutes or until al dente, then drain thoroughly.
2. Meanwhile, fill a microwave-safe bowl with water. Add the asparagus and microwave on high for three minutes or until tender-crisp.
3. Mix the garlic, cherry tomatoes, basil and pepper in a large mixing bowl. Stir in the cooked pasta along with the asparagus and goat cheese.
4. Allow the pasta mixture to chill in the refrigerator for about twenty minutes.
5. Serve chilled pasta on individual plates. Add fresh basil leaves on top and enjoy.

Serving size = 2 ½ cups
Servings: 2
Nutrition Information: 64 g total carbohydrate, 10 g dietary fiber, 142 mg sodium, 4 g saturated fat, 8 g total fat, 0 g trans fat, 13 mg cholesterol, 17g protein, 1 g monounsaturated fat, 396 calories, 0 g added sugars.

Chapter 5 – Weight Loss-Inducing Turkey, Pork and Beef Recipes

To help you achieve your goal of becoming healthier and shedding off excess weight, it is important to realize that you need to lower your calorie intake. This is why the DASH Diet is your best bet to effective weight loss: It helps you eat less sodium and also encourages you to eat more of naturally low-calorie foods that are prepared with healthy ingredients and cooking methods.

MAIN DISH - TURKEY

Glazed Fruit-Stuffed Turkey

Ingredients:
Turkey breast, bone-in, whole, five-pound, thawed (1 piece)
Stuffing:
Cranberries, dried (1/4 cup)
Onion, small, sliced thinly (1 piece)
Pear, peeled, sliced thinly (1 piece)
Apple, peeled, sliced thinly (1 piece)
Rub:
Thyme leaves, fresh, chopped (2 tablespoons)
Rosemary, fresh, chopped (2 tablespoons)
Olive oil, extra virgin (2 tablespoons)
Glaze:
Mustard, brown (1 tablespoon)
Apple juice (1 cup + 1 cup)
Olive oil, extra virgin (1 tablespoon)
Sugar, brown (1 tablespoon)

Directions:

1. Set the oven at 325 degrees to preheat. Meanwhile, set the turkey breast on a roasting pan's rack with its skin-side up.

2. Mix the olive oil and herbs in a small mixing bowl, making sure the mixture turns into a paste.

3. Use your fingers to gently loosen the meat from its skin until two deep pockets are made. Spread ½ of the paste directly on the turkey meat. Smear the rest of the paste on the turkey skin surface.

4. In a separate bowl, combine the cranberries, pear slices, apple slices and onions. Fill the two turkey meat pockets with the fruit-onion mixture, then loosely cover with aluminum foil (this helps keep the meat from over-browning in the oven).

5. Add apple juice (1 cup) to the roasting pan. Place in the oven to roast for two hours or until the turkey's internal temperature registers 165 degrees and its skin becomes golden brown.

6. Meanwhile, mix the apple juice (1 cup) with the olive oil, mustard and brown sugar in a saucepan. Heat on medium-high and allow the mixture to boil. Lower heat to medium-low and let the mixture simmer to thicken it (its volume should be reduced to ¾ cup). Set aside for using later in basting the turkey while it is in its last half-hour of cooking.

7. Once the turkey is cooked, let stand at room temperature for about fifteen minutes. Remove the foil and carve.

8. Serve turkey topped with any remaining glaze.

Serving size = 6-ounce portion
Servings: 12
Nutrition Information: 15 g total carbohydrate, 1 g dietary fiber, 112 mg sodium, 4 g saturated fat, 14 g

total fat, 100 mg cholesterol, 40 g protein, 2 g monounsaturated fat, 346 calories.

Juicy Herb Turkey

Ingredients:
Olive oil, extra virgin (1 tablespoon)
Turkey, whole, 15 pounds, thawed (1 piece)
Water (1/2 cup)
Rub:
Sage, dried (2 teaspoons)
Parsley, fresh, chopped (2 tablespoons)
Thyme, dried (1 tablespoon)
Au jus:
Apple juice (1/2 cup)
Thyme, dried (1 tablespoon)
Sage, dried (2 teaspoons)
Honey (2 tablespoons)
Pan drippings, defatted (1 cup)
Parsley, fresh, chopped (2 tablespoons)

Directions:
1. Set the oven to 325 degrees to preheat. Meanwhile, place the parsley, thyme and sage in a small mixing bowl. Combine and set aside.
2. Discard the turkey's neck and giblets. Use cool water to rinse the turkey thoroughly inside-out.
3. After patting dry the turkey with paper towels, gently loosen its skin from the meat with your fingers. Set on a roasting pan's rack before adding some herb mixture (1 tablespoon) underneath the skin.
4. Use olive oil to coat the surface of the turkey before rubbing with the rest of the herb mixture.
5. After loosely tying the legs of the turkey together, place in the oven (at the center) to cook for 1 ½ hours. Keep from overcooking by covering with a foil tent. Roast further for another three hours or until the juices run clear and the breast part registers 175 degrees.

6. Take the turkey roast out of the oven and let stand for about twenty minutes. While the juices are settling in the meat, add water (1/2 cup) to the pan. Stir to deglaze and then pour the drippings into the grave separator. Set aside one cup for your au jus.

7. Pour the apple juice into a separate saucepan. Add the honey, thyme, parsley and sage, then mix well. Allow mixture to simmer on medium until its volume is reduced by ½. Stir in the set-aside drippings and allow to boil on low, making sure to stir often.

8. After carving the turkey, drizzle with the prepared au jus.

9. Serve right away.

Serving size = 4 ounces meat (light & dark)
Servings: 10
Nutrition Information: 5 g total carbohydrate, trace dietary fiber, 91 mg sodium, 1 g saturated fat, 3 g total fat, 0 g trans fat, 117 mg cholesterol, 37 g protein, 1 g monounsaturated fat, 215 calories, 3 g added sugars.

Turkey Casserole on Toast

Ingredients:
Flour, all-purpose/plain (3 tablespoons)
Onions, diced (1/3 cup)
Black pepper, ground (1/2 teaspoon)
Celery, diced (1/2 cup)
Parsley, fresh, chopped (1/2 cup)
Rosemary, fresh (2 tablespoons)
Chicken broth, low-sodium (1 ½ cups)
Turkey, cubed, cooked (2 cups)
Wine, white (3 tablespoons)
Toast, whole wheat (4 slices)
Bell pepper, green, seeded, chopped (1/2 piece)

Directions:
1. Heat a large saucepan (nonstick) on medium-high. Add chicken broth (1/4 cup) and allow to simmer.
 2. Stir in onions, bell pepper and celery. Cook for about four to five minutes or until the veggies are tender-crisp.
3. Lower heat and allow mixture to simmer while cooling slightly.
4. Meanwhile, place the cubed turkey and flour in a large mixing bowl. Gently toss until the meat is evenly coated with the flour.
5. Pour the mixture into the saucepan and combine with the broth and vegetables. Turn the heat back up to medium-high and gradually stir in the wine, remaining broth, black pepper, rosemary and parsley.
6. Stir continuously for five minutes or until the entire mixture slightly thickens. Serve ¼ of the prepared casserole on top of each toast.

Serving size = ¼ portion of casserole w/ 1 slice of toast
Servings: 4

Nutrition Information: 23 g total carbohydrate, 4 g dietary fiber, 237 mg sodium, 1 g saturated fat, 4 g total fat, trace trans fat, 71 mg cholesterol, 27 g protein, 2 g monounsaturated fat, 236 calories, 0 g added sugars.

MAIN DISH – PORK

Superb Pork Tenderloin

Ingredients:
Pork tenderloin, cut into four-ounce portions (4 pieces)
Cayenne pepper (1/8 teaspoon)
Cinnamon, ground (1/8 teaspoon)
Cumin, ground (1/4 teaspoon)
Coriander, ground (1 teaspoon)
Sesame seeds (2 tablespoons)
Celery seed (1/8 teaspoon)
Onion, minced (1/2 teaspoon)
Sesame oil (1 tablespoon)

Directions:
1. Set the oven to 400 degrees to preheat. Meanwhile, use cooking spray to coat the baking dish lightly.
2. Heat a frying pan (heavy-bottomed) on low before adding the sesame seeds, making sure they form a single layer. Cook and stir for about one to two minutes or until they have a toasty aroma and a golden color. Take out of the pan and set aside to cool.
3. Place the sesame oil in a large bowl. Add the toasted sesame seeds, celery seed, coriander, minced onion, cinnamon, cayenne pepper and cumin. Stir well to combine.
4. After placing the pork in the baking dish, rub both sides with the sesame oil mixture. Place in the oven to bake for fifteen minutes or until the meat is no longer pink and its internal temperature registers 165 to 170 degrees.
5. Serve pork tenderloin immediately on warmed plates.

Serving size = 1 piece
Servings: 4
Nutrition Information: trace total carbohydrate, 0 g dietary fiber, 57 mg sodium, 5 g saturated fat, 16 g total fat, trace trans fat, 61 mg cholesterol, 26 g protein, 7 g monounsaturated fat, 248 calories, 0 g added sugars.

Hot Grilled Pork Fajitas

Ingredients:
Tortillas, whole wheat, 8-inch diameter, microwave-warmed (8 pieces)
Paprika (1/2 teaspoon)
Tomatoes, medium, diced (4 pieces)
Oregano (1/2 teaspoon)
Cheddar cheese, sharp, shredded (1/2 cup)
Lettuce, shredded (4 cups)
Chili powder (1 tablespoon)
Garlic powder (1/4 teaspoon)
Onion, small, diced (1 piece)
Salsa (1 cup)
Coriander, ground (1/4 teaspoon)
Pork tenderloin, sliced into ½-inch-wide & 2-inch long strips (1 pound)

Directions:
1. Set the broiler to 400 degrees to preheat.
2. Meanwhile, place the coriander, oregano, chili powder, garlic powder, and paprika in a small mixing bowl. Use this mixture to completely coat the pork pieces.
3. Transfer the seasoned pork strips into a grill basket. Add the onions and cook for about five minutes or until completely browned.
4. Top each warmed tortilla with 1/8 of the onions and pork strips, cheese (1 tablespoon), shredded lettuce (1/2 cup), tomatoes (2 tablespoons), and salsa (2 tablespoons).
5. Fold and roll to close each tortilla, then serve right away.

Serving size = 1 fajita
Servings: 8

Nutrition Information: 29 g total carbohydrate, 10 g dietary fiber, 535 mg sodium, 2 g saturated fat, 6 g total fat, trace trans fat, 45 mg cholesterol, 20 g protein, 1.5 g monounsaturated fat, 250 calories, 5 g added sugars.

Fennel Pork Tenderloin

Ingredients:
Olive oil, extra virgin (2 tablespoons)
Chicken broth, low-sodium (12 ounces)
Fennel bulb, cored, sliced thinly (1 piece)
Pork tenderloin, filleted, 4-ounce (4 pieces)
Sweet onion, sliced thinly (1 piece)
Fennel fronds (a pinch)
White wine, dry (1/2 cup)
Orange slices (a pinch)
Fennel seeds (1 teaspoon)

Directions:
1. Arrange the pork between layers of wax paper. Use a mallet to pound the meat until it is about a quarter-inch thick.
2. Heat a heavy skillet (nonstick) on medium before adding the oil. Stir in the fennel seeds and cook for about three minutes or until fragrant.
3. Stir in the pork and cook for another three minutes or until the meat is completely browned.
4. Take the pork out of the skillet and set aside in a covered dish to keep warm.
5. Add the sliced onion and fennel to the skillet. Cook for about five minutes or until tender. Take the veggie mixture out of the skillet and set aside in another covered dish to keep warm.
6. Pour the chicken broth and wine into the skillet. Allow the mixture to boil on high. Once reduced in half, add the warm pork and cover. Reduce heat to low and cook for five minutes before adding the onion and fennel mixture.
7. Cover and allow mixture to cook for an additional two minutes.
8. Transfer onto warmed plates. Garnish with orange slices and fennel fronds.

9. Serve and enjoy.

Serving size = 1 piece w/ veggies
Servings: 4
Nutrition Information: 13 g total carbohydrate, 3 g dietary fiber, 122 mg sodium, 3 g saturated fat, 12 g total fat, 0 g trans fat, 71 mg cholesterol, 29 g protein, 9 g monounsaturated fat, 276 calories, 7 g total sugars, 0 g added sugars.

MAIN DISH – BEEF

Stewed Beef

Ingredients:
White potato, w/ skin, diced (1/2 cup)
Stock, beef/vegetable, low-sodium (3 cups)
Yellow onions, diced (2 cups)
Parsley, fresh, minced (1 tablespoon)
Canola oil (2 teaspoons)
Balsamic vinegar (1 teaspoon)
Carrot, diced (1 cup)
Rosemary, dried, minced (1 teaspoon)
Mushrooms, diced (1/2 cup)
Thyme, fresh, minced (1 teaspoon)
Garlic, chopped (4 cloves)
Oregano, dried (1 tablespoon)
Celery, diced (1 cup)
Sage, dried, crushed (1 teaspoon)
Sweet potato, diced (1/2 cup)
Beef steak, round (1 pound)
Barley, uncooked (1/4 cup)
Vinegar, red wine (1/4 cup)
Kale, chopped (1 cup)
Black pepper (1/2 teaspoon)
Tomatoes, Roma, diced (1 cup)

Directions:
1. Place steak in preheated (medium) broiler or grill. Cook for about twelve to fourteen minutes. Once done, set aside to cool.
2. Heat a large pot on medium-high. Add the oil and vegetables. Cook for about ten minutes or until lightly browned.
3. Stir in the barley and cook for another five minutes. Meanwhile, use paper towels to pat the meat dry.

4. After dicing the grilled steak into ½-inch cubes, add to the pot along with the stock, vinegars, spices and herbs.

5. Allow the mixture to simmer and cook for about one hour or until the barley is thoroughly cooked and the stew is considerably thick.

Serving size = 2 cups
Servings: 4
Nutrition Information: 35 g total carbohydrate, 7 g dietary fiber, 166 mg sodium, 2 g saturated fat, 9 g total fat, 0 g trans fat, 84 mg cholesterol, 42 g protein, 4 g monounsaturated fat, 389 calories, 0 g added sugars.

Easy Beef Stoganoff

Ingredients:

Soup, cream of mushroom, fat-free, undiluted (1/2 can)

Sour cream, fat-free (1/2 cup)

Beef steak, round, boneless, ¾-inch thick, trimmed of all fat (1/2 pound)

 Flour, all-purpose/plain (1 tablespoon)

Onion, chopped (1/2 cup)

Egg noodles, yolkless, uncooked (4 cups)

Water (1/2 cup)

Paprika (1/2 teaspoon)

Directions:

1. Heat a frying pan (nonstick) on medium before adding the onions. Sauté for about five minutes or until the onions are translucent.

2. Stir in the beef. Cook for an additional five minutes or until beef is tender and completely browned. Drain the beef thoroughly before setting aside.

3. Meanwhile, pour water into a large pot until it is ¾ full. Allow to boil before adding the noodles. Cook for ten to twelve minutes or until al dente, then drain thoroughly.

4. Heat a saucepan on medium heat before adding the flour, soup and water. Whisk well to combine and cook for five minutes or until thickened.

5. Pour the prepared sauce into the frying pan. Add paprika and cook on medium. Stir well. Once warmed through, remove from the stove and mix in the sour cream.

5. Serve pasta topped with the prepared beef mixture and enjoy.

Serving size = 2 ½ cups
Servings: 4

Nutrition Information: 37 g total carbohydrate, 2 g dietary fiber, 193 mg sodium, 2 g saturated fat, 5 g total fat, trace trans fat, 82 mg cholesterol, 20 g protein, 2 g monounsaturated fat, 273 calories, 0 g added sugars.

Delectable Beef Brisket

Ingredients:
Onions, chopped (1 ½ cups)
Vinegar, red wine (1/4 cup)
Tomatoes, w/ liquid, no-salt-added (14.5 ounces)
Pepper, coarsely ground (1/2 teaspoon)
Olive oil (1 tablespoon)
Garlic, smashed, peeled (4 cloves)
Thyme, dried (1 teaspoon)
Beef stock, low-sodium (1 cup)
Beef brisket, sliced into 8 equal portions (2 ½ pounds)

Directions:
1. Set the oven to 350 degrees to preheat. Meanwhile, heat on medium a heavy pot or large Dutch oven while seasoning the brisket with pepper.
2. Add to oil (1 tablespoon) to the pot. Once heated, add the seasoned brisket as well. Cook until all sides are browned, then transfer onto a plate.
3. Cook onions in the same pot. Once onions are browned, stir in thyme and garlic. Cook for about one minute or until fragrant.
4. Pour wine/stock into the pot, along with the vinegar and tomatoes (undrained). Allow the mixture to boil before placing the beef back in the pot. Cover and cook for about three to 3 ½ hours or until meat is tender.
5. Serve right away.

Serving size = 3 ounces meat + 3 ounces sauce
Servings: 8
Nutrition Information: 6 g total carbohydrate, 1 g dietary fiber, 184 mg sodium, 3 g saturated fat, 9 g total fat, trace trans fat, 95 mg cholesterol, 31 g protein, 5 g monounsaturated fat, 229 calories, 0 g added sugars.

Conclusion

Thank you again for reading this book!

I hope this book was able to help you to see how easy it is to adopt the DASH Diet as part of your long-term plan to live a healthy and lean life.

The next step is to seek the support of your doctor or other health professionals in helping you to commit to the DASH Diet, especially if you are having a hard time sticking to it. It also helps to reduce your intake of alcohol (men: 2 drinks or less; women: 1 drink or less), which can cause raised blood pressure levels. It would also be in your best interest to avoid coffee, which can temporarily elevate blood pressure.

Finally, if you enjoyed this book, please take the time to share your thoughts and post a review on Amazon. It'd be greatly appreciated!

Thank you and good luck!

Manuscript 2:
DASH Diet
The DASH Diet Guide with Delicious DASH Recipes for Weight Loss

Introduction

Are you suffering from high blood pressure? Or does your family's health history reveal that you have high risk of developing it? If so, then you need to take charge of your health and habits now so that you can extend the length and enhance the quality of your life. The best and easiest way to begin stabilizing your blood pressure levels is by following the DASH Diet.

DASH, or *Dietary Approaches to Stop Hypertension*, is a simple, straightforward and practical guide on how to prevent or treat high blood pressure. The guidelines are so simple that you can immediately start applying it right now, and this book is here to help you out.

In this book, you will find a quick and easy guide to following the DASH diet. You will also gain 50 delicious DASH-approved recipes for not just improving your blood pressure levels, but also helping you to lose weight the healthy way. You will find recipes for breakfast, main dishes – be they for lunch or dinner – side dishes that can also serve as snacks, and desserts.

The great thing about these recipes is you can find the exact amount of grams per serving size and the nutritional information per serving. That way, you will know exactly how much protein, fat, and carbohydrates you are consuming, and you can tweak the ingredients depending on your health goals. In addition, all of the recipes in this book call for ingredients you can conveniently find in your local grocery store or farmer's market. You can also easily choose alternatives to the ingredients in times when they are not in season.

So take control over your quality of life now by implementing the DASH diet. Start by turning to Chapter 1.

Chapter 1 – A Short Guide to the DASH Diet

DASH is the acronym for "Dietary Approaches to Stop Hypertension," and it means exactly that. If you have a family health history of hypertension, suspect that you have it, or that you are diagnosed with it, then it is best for you to adopt the DASH diet into your lifestyle right now.

But before we head on over to discussing the DASH Diet guidelines, let us first take a look at what hypertension is.

What is Hypertension?

Hypertension, otherwise known as high blood pressure, is a health disorder in which the blood pressure stays at an abnormally high level, or at least 140/90 mm Hg. It affects almost a third of the entire adult population in the United States and in other countries that follow the conventional western type of diet – one that is rich in sodium and fat.

The worst part about hypertension is that some people are unaware they have it. Thus, they would continue to eat these unhealthy foods and would stop only when more a more critical health issue caused by their underlying hypertension arises, such as stroke, coronary artery disease (or CAD), angina, and heart failure.

While these facts presented to you are not meant to scare you, they are there to help inspire you to start the DASH diet, which is low in sodium and fat and rich in healthy, naturally sourced proteins and carbs.

DASH Diet: Regular and DASH Sodium

There are two types of DASH diet, one of which is called the Regular DASH Diet and the other, DASH Sodium.

The idea is simple: if you are someone who do not have hypertension but may be at risk of it due the results of a blood pressure test, or due to your family's health history of it, then you can follow the Regular DASH Diet. In this diet, you can still incorporate sodium into your life such as by using small amounts of Himalayan sea salt and other healthier salts. The salt to avoid is table salt.

On the other hand, if you are already diagnosed with hypertension, then you need to follow the DASH Sodium. In this diet, you should avoid sodium entirely and make sure that your meals do not contain any salt unless they are a natural component of a particular ingredient. Those who are on the DASH Sodium should also control their intake of foods naturally high in sodium, such as artichokes, beets, carrots, turnips, raw celeriac, wax gourd, chard, celery, sweet potatoes, spinach, and collards.

If you are not sure yet as to whether you have hypertension or not, you should visit your doctor to have yourself tested. What he will do is to review your medical history first, then conduct a physical examination. Aside from a blood pressure reading, you may also be advised to take a cholesterol test together with blood tests and a urine test.

Normal blood pressure is one that is below 120/80 mm Hg. If yours has a 120 to 139 mm Hg systolic pressure or 80 to 89 mm Hg diastolic pressure, then you are considered to have "prehypertension," or a high risk of developing hypertension. If your systolic pressure is between 140 and 159 mm Hg and your diastolic pressure is 90 to 99 mm Hg, then you have "Stage 1 Hypertension." Those with "Stage 2 Hypertension" have a systolic pressure of at least 160 mm Hg or a diastolic pressure of at least 100 mm Hg.

Take note that those over the age of 60 years old have significantly higher levels of systolic reading, thus is it not unnatural to have a diastolic pressure that is less than 90 mm Hg and a systolic pressure of at least 141 mm Hg if you are around that age.

That being said, those who are in the Prehypertension stage should follow the Regular DASH diet and those who are in Stage 1 or 2 Hypertension should strictly follow DASH Sodium.

DASH Diet Guidelines

The DASH Diet is far from restrictive when it comes to the variety of foods you can eat. There are so many healthy vegetables, fruits, nuts, seeds, and other delicious, low-sodium and low-fat meals you can enjoy every day. And when you are in doubt, then just call to mind the following five simple DASH Diet guidelines:

1. Learn to love food sans added salt.

Sodium significantly reduces your kidneys' function to eliminate water from your body. Due to the retention of extra fluid and strain on the blood vessels, your blood pressure will increase. Since salt *is* sodium, it is best to avoid it entirely and use black pepper – which helps lower blood pressure – instead.

2. Always serve vegetables with every lunch and dinner meal.

Vegetables are rich in fiber and nutrients, but many people especially those who are used to the conventional western diet do not get enough of it. By making it a point to serve vegetables with each main meal, you guarantee yourself a well-balanced diet and a reduced risk of not only hypertension but also of other chronic disease.

3. **Do not consume more than 6 ounces of meat per day.**

Meat, especially red meat such as pork and beef and processed meat, is considered to be unsafe to those who have prehypertension and hypertension due to their high LDL cholesterol content. Processed meat in particular is especially high in sodium and should be cut out entirely. As often as possible, choose to have fatty fish such as salmon and sardines and white meat such as chicken and turkey.

4. **Choose skim or low-fat dairy products, otherwise cut them out entirely and use organic vegan alternatives such as almond milk.**

Whole milk is rich in saturated fat, with a cup containing 8 grams of fat, 58 percent of which is saturated fat. The American Heart Association advises everyone, whether they have hypertension or not, to limit saturated fat in whole milk, butter, cheese, and red meat as these can increase your risk of heart disease.

5. **Fresh fruit can be eaten as a snack or as a dessert after meals.**

Fresh fruit is the best alternative to conventional desserts and snacks for although they are rich in sugar, they are also rich in fiber, vitamins, minerals, and antioxidants. So go ahead and snack on an apple when your sweet tooth craves for a treat.

Top 12 Foods that Aggravate Hypertension

If there are any foods you should keep away from at all costs, then this is the list you can refer to. The reason why these foods should be avoided is that they are dangerously high in sodium and LDL cholesterol for those who have prehypertension or hypertension.

1. Pickles and Sauerkraut

2. Table Salt

3. Canned soups

4. Deep-fried food such as French fries and donuts

5. Frozen foods

6. Bacon

7. Red meat

8. Whole Milk

9. Margarine

10. Packaged noodles

11. Refined Sugar

12. Alcohol

Top 25 Foods that Help Reduce Hypertension

As there are foods that worsen hypertension, so too are their foods that can help to reduce it. These foods are rich in natural vitamins, minerals, and enzymes that help to lower blood pressure levels. Make sure to incorporate a wide variety of them into your meals.

1. Leafy Greens, such as kale and spinach
2. Broccoli
3. Red Bell Pepper
4. Garlic
5. Turmeric
6. Cinnamon
7. Sweet Potato
8. Quinoa
9. Whole Grains
10. Flaxseeds
11. Traditional Rolled Oats
12. Fatty Fish
13. Low- or Non-Fat Plain Greek Yogurt
14. Beets
15. Extra Virgin Olive Oil
16. Pistachios

17. Almonds

18. Cashews

19. Berries

20. Avocado

21. Kiwifruit

22. Bananas

23. Hibiscus Tea

24. Green Tea

25. White Beans

Chapter 2 – DASH Breakfast and Brunch Recipes

Poached Eggs and Spinach

Number of Servings: 3

Ingredients:

- 3 eggs
- 3 egg whites
- 3 cups fresh baby spinach leaves
- 3 tsp. olive oil
- Ground nutmeg, to taste
- Ground paprika, to taste
- Freshly ground black pepper, to taste

How to Prepare:

Lightly coat the inside of three ramekins with olive oil.

Arrange the ramekins in a large pot and pour water around them, taking care not to let any water into the ramekins.

Break one egg into each ramekin then divide the egg whites. Cover the pot and bring to a boil. Cook until the eggs are poached and set.

Divide the baby spinach among the poached eggs and season with nutmeg, paprika, and black pepper. Let stand until the baby spinach is wilted. Serve warm.

Nutritional Information per Serving:

138 grams per 1 serving

Energy (calories): 193 kcal

Protein: 13 g

Fat: 14 g

Carbohydrates: 2 g

Whole Grain Cinnamon Toast with Banana and Nut Butter

Number of Servings: 2

Ingredients:

- 4 slices whole wheat bread
- 4 Tbsp. nut butter, such as almond
- 2 bananas
- ¼ tsp. ground cinnamon

How to Prepare:

Lightly toast the 4 slices of whole wheat bread.

In the meantime, peel the bananas then slice them into thin rounds. Set aside.

Once the toasted slices are ready, spread the nut butter on one side of each and sprinkle the ground cinnamon on top. Lay the sliced banana over each slice, then serve right away.

Nutritional Information per Serving:

265 grams per 1 serving

Energy (calories): 509 kcal

Protein: 16 g

Fat: 20 g

Carbohydrates: 72 g

Warm Cilantro Hummus Stuffed Pitas

Number of Servings: 3

Ingredients:

- 1 ½ whole wheat pitas, 7 inches each
- 1 small garlic clove
- 1 roasted red bell pepper
- ¼ cup chopped cilantro leaves
- ½ cup baby spinach leaves
- ¼ cup canned or cooked chickpeas
- ¾ Tbsp. freshly squeezed lime juice
- ¾ Tbsp. olive oil

How to Prepare:

Rinse and drain the chickpeas thoroughly then set aside.

Set the oven to 350 degrees F to preheat.

Core, stem, and halve the bell pepper then roast in the oven until tender, about 5 minutes.

Meanwhile, combine the cilantro, chickpeas, spinach, olive oil, and lime juice in a food processor. Blend until smooth.

Remove the bell pepper from the oven and chop into thin strips. Set aside.

Divide the hummus among the pita halves then stuff with the chopped bell pepper and spinach.

Arrange the stuffed pitas on a baking sheet and bake for 8 to 10 minutes, or until warmed through and crisp. Slice into bite-sized pieces and serve.

Nutritional Information per Serving:

57 grams per 1 serving

Energy (calories): 100 kcal

Protein: 3 g

Fat: 4 g

Carbohydrates: 14 g

Berry Oatmeal

Number of Servings: 3

Ingredients:

- 2 cups low- or non-fat dairy or nut milk
- 1 ½ cups traditional rolled oats
- 1 ¼ cups mixed berries, such as blueberries, raspberries, and blackberries
- 3 Tbsp. toasted pistachios or almonds
- 1/3 tsp. pure vanilla extract

How to Prepare:

Combine the milk and vanilla extract in a saucepan then place over low flame. Stir until heated through, but do not bring to a simmer.

Once the milk is hot, stir in the rolled oats. Continue to stir until the rolled oats are warm and tender to a desired consistency. Add more milk, if needed.

Divide the oatmeal into three servings and top with the berries and toasted nuts. Serve right away.

Nutritional Information per Serving:

308 grams per 1 serving

Energy (calories): 437 kcal

Protein: 18 g

Fat: 14 g

Carbohydrates: 80 g

Curried Sweet Potato Hash Browns

Number of Servings: 3

Ingredients:

- 1 small onion
- 2 eggs
- 6 cups baby spinach
- 2 cups peeled and grated sweet potato
- ¼ cup fine yellow cornmeal
- ¼ cup frozen green peas, thawed
- 2 Tbsp. freshly squeezed lemon juice
- 1 Tbsp. curry powder
- ½ tsp. freshly grated ginger
- Freshly ground black pepper, to taste

How to Prepare:

Peel and finely dice the onion then set aside.

Beat the eggs together with the ginger, curry powder, and cornmeal. Fold in the grated sweet potato, green peas, and diced onion. Mix well.

Season the mixture with onion powder and black pepper, then aside.

Place a nonstick skillet over medium flame and heat through. Once hot, add the olive oil and swirl to coat. Add about ¼ cup of the sweet potato mixture on the hot skillet and reduce to medium low flame. Cook for 4 minutes per side, or until golden brown and crisp.

Place the hash browns on a platter and repeat with the remaining batter.

Once the hashed browns are cooked, wipe the skillet clean and add the spinach with about a tablespoon of water. Cook until wilted, then divide into three servings.

Divide the hash browns among the three servings then sprinkle with lemon juice and serve right away.

Nutritional Information per Serving:

256 grams per 1 serving

Energy (calories): 11 kcal

Protein: 11 g

Fat: 7 g

Carbohydrates: 37 g

Berry Coconut Quinoa Breakfast Bowls

Number of Servings: 6

Ingredients:

- 1 ¾ cups coconut milk, unsweetened
- 1 ½ cups raw quinoa
- 1 ½ cups water
- ¾ cups mixed berries, such as blackberries or blueberries
- 3 Tbsp. chopped pistachios or almonds
- (Optional) 3 tsp. raw honey or pure maple syrup

How to Prepare:

Pour the quinoa into a fine mesh strainer and rinse thoroughly under cold running water until the water runs clear. Drain well then transfer into a saucepan.

Pour the coconut milk and water into the quinoa and stir to combine. Place the pot over high flame, cover, and bring to a boil.

Once boiling, reduce to low flame and simmer for 10 minutes or until the quinoa is almost tender and has absorbed most of the liquid.

Remove the quinoa from the heat and set aside, covered, for 5 minutes. After that, uncover and fluff up the quinoa using a fork.

Divide the quinoa into three servings and add the berries, chopped nuts, and honey or maple syrup (if using) on top. Serve right away, stirring before eating.

Nutritional Information per Serving:

206 grams per 1 serving

Energy (calories): 410 kcal

Protein: 9 g

Fat: 23 g

Carbohydrates: 46 g

Buckwheat Flapjacks with Berries and Cottage Cheese

Number of Servings: 5

Ingredients:

- 4 oz. low fat cottage cheese

- 1 large egg

- 1 cup fresh berries, such as blueberries, raspberries, and/or blackberries

- ½ cup low-fat milk

- ¼ cup whole wheat flour

- ¼ cup buckwheat flour

- 1 Tbsp. avocado, grapeseed, or sunflower oil

- ½ Tbsp. pure maple syrup

- ½ tsp. pure vanilla extract

How to Prepare:

Whisk together the egg, 1 tablespoon of oil, ½ tablespoon of pure maple syrup, and pure vanilla extract. Mix well.

Sift the whole wheat and buckwheat flours into the egg mixture followed by the low fat milk and mix until just combined; do not over-mix or this will cause the flapjacks to be rubbery.

Cover the bowl and let stand for half an hour to thicken slightly.

Once the batter is ready, place a nonstick skillet over medium flame and heat through. Add about 1 ½ tablespoons of the batter on the hot skillet and cook for about 1 minute per side, or until firm. Transfer to a platter and repeat with the remaining batter.

Divide the flapjacks into five servings and spoon the cottage cheese on top. Add the berries and serve right away.

Nutritional Information per Serving:

137 grams per 1 serving

Energy (calories): 334 kcal

Protein: 14 g

Fat: 17 g

Carbohydrates: 32 g

Herbed Garlic Tofu Scramble

Number of Servings: 6

Ingredients:

- 21 oz. firm tofu
- 5 green onions
- 4 garlic cloves
- 1 ½ cups mung bean sprouts
- 3 Tbsp. chopped fresh mint
- 3 Tbsp. chopped fresh flat leaf parsley
- 2 Tbsp. olive oil
- 1 ½ Tbsp. freshly squeezed lime juice
- Freshly ground black pepper, to taste

How to Prepare:

Peel and dice the garlic and set aside. Chop the green onions and set aside.

Drain the tofu thoroughly then dice into small pieces and set aside.

Place a nonstick skillet over medium flame and heat through. Once hot, add the olive oil and swirl to coat. Sauté the garlic until fragrant, then add the tofu and green onions and cook, stirring occasionally, until warmed through.

Add the mung bean sprouts and sauté until warmed through. Then, add the lime juice, parsley, and mint. Stir well to combine.

Transfer the tofu scramble to a platter and serve right away.

Nutritional Information per Serving:

219 grams per 1 serving

Energy (calories): 361 kcal

Protein: 37 g

Fat: 22 g

Carbohydrates: 7 g

Banana Almond Oat Pancakes

Number of Servings: 3

Ingredients:

- 1 whole egg
- 1 egg white
- 1 large banana
- 1 ¼ cups traditional rolled oats
- 1 cup almond milk, unsweetened
- 2 ½ Tbsp. applesauce, unsweetened
- ½ tsp. ground cinnamon

How to Prepare:

Peel the banana then place in a bowl and mash well. Add the egg and egg white, followed by the almond milk and ground cinnamon, then mix well until smooth.

Fold in the rolled oats and applesauce, stirring until evenly combined and pasty.

Place a nonstick skillet over low flame and heat through. Add three tablespoons of the batter onto the skillet, spreading out into the shape of a pancake.

Cook for 1 minute per side, or until firm. Transfer to a plate and repeat with the remaining batter.

Serve right away.

Nutritional Information per Serving:

212 grams per 1 serving

Energy (calories): 232 kcal

Protein: 12 g

Fat: 7 g

Carbohydrates: 46 g

Egg Florentine

Number of Servings: 3

Ingredients:

- 3 eggs
- 3 egg whites
- 4 cups chopped spinach
- 4 cups water
- ½ cup low fat milk
- 1 Tbsp. whole wheat flour
- ¾ Tbsp. white vinegar
- ¾ Tbsp. nut butter
- Ground nutmeg, to taste
- Freshly ground black pepper, to taste

How to Prepare:

Place the spinach into a saucepan and cook until wilted. Set aside in a bowl.

Place a small skillet, add the nut butter and milk and stir until melted. Turn off the heat then stir in the flour until smooth. Season to taste with nutmeg and black pepper, then mix in the spinach. Divide into three servings and set aside.

In the same saucepan, combine the water and vinegar. Bring to a boil over high flame. Add the eggs and egg whites and cook until set. Carefully remove the poached eggs and egg whites from the boiling water and divide among the spinach servings. Serve right away.

Nutritional Information per Serving:

510 grams per 1 serving

Energy (calories): 210 kcal

Protein: 16 g

Fat: 13 g

Carbohydrates: 8 g

Artichoke Oregano Egg Scramble

Number of Servings: 2

Ingredients:

- 2 whole eggs
- 4 organic egg whites
- 1 red onion
- 2 large garlic cloves
- 1 small red bell pepper
- ½ cup finely chopped artichoke hearts
- ¼ cup low fat feta cheese
- 2 Tbsp. avocado, grape seed, or sunflower oil
- 1/4 Tbsp. fresh oregano (or ¼ tsp. dried)
- Freshly ground black pepper, to taste

How to Prepare:

Peel and dice the onion and garlic, then set aside.

Stem, core, and seed the bell pepper, then chop into tiny bits and set aside.

Place a large nonstick skillet over medium flame and heat through. Once hot, add the oil and swirl to coat.

And sauté the onion until translucent. Then, add the garlic and sauté until fragrant.

Stir in the bell pepper until tender then add the artichoke hearts and sauté until crisp tender.

Add the eggs and egg whites into the skillet with the vegetables and scramble until almost cooked. After that, stir in the fresh or dried oregano with a pinch of black pepper. Mix well until the eggs are set to a desired consistency.

Turn off the heat then transfer the scramble to a platter. Top with feta cheese and let melt before serving. Best served warm.

Nutritional Information per Serving:

288 grams per 1 serving

Energy (calories): 371 kcal

Protein: 23 g

Fat: 25 g

Carbohydrates: 14 g

Peanut Butter Banana Breakfast Wraps

Number of Servings: 3

Ingredients:

- 2 bananas

- 3 whole wheat tortillas

- 6 Tbsp. all natural peanut butter

- 6 Tbsp. organic granola

- 3 Tbsp. raisins

- ¾ tsp. ground cinnamon

How to Prepare:

Thinly slice the bananas. Spread the peanut butter on the tortillas then sprinkle the granola on top of each. Add the banana slices, followed by the raisins and cinnamon.

Roll up and place on a microwaveable platter. Microwave for 10 seconds then serve.

Nutritional Information per Serving:

172 grams per 1 serving

Energy (calories): 462 kcal

Protein: 16 g

Fat: 20 g

Carbohydrates: 58 g

Vegetable Medley Egg Scramble

Number of Servings: 3

Ingredients:

- 2 whole eggs
- 2 organic egg whites
- 1 large garlic clove
- 1 small red onion
- 1 small red bell pepper
- 1 cup mixed greens, such as kale, spinach, and collard greens
- ¼ cup chopped broccoli
- 1 Tbsp. avocado, grape seed, or sunflower oil
- 1 Tbsp. water
- Freshly ground black pepper, to taste

How to Prepare:

Place the greens in a colander and rinse well under cold running water. Squeeze out excess water, chop, and set aside.

Peel and dice the onion and garlic clove, then set aside.

Stem, core, and seed the bell pepper, then chop into small bits and set aside.

Place a large nonstick skillet over medium flame and heat   through.
Add the oil and swirl to coat. Stir in the mixed greens and sauté for about 3 minutes, or until wilted. Then, add the water, broccoli, garlic, onion, and bell pepper.

Cover the skillet and cook for about 2 minutes or until the vegetables are all tender.

In the meantime, whisk the egg whites and whole eggs in a bowl with a pinch of black pepper. Set aside.

Once the vegetables are ready, uncover the skillet and stir in the egg mixture. Scramble well until eggs are cooked to a desired consistency, set but not rubbery, and vegetables are crisp tender.

Transfer to a platter and serve right away.

Nutritional Information per Serving:

142 grams per 1 serving

Energy (calories): 200 kcal

Protein: 9 g

Fat: 16 g

Carbohydrates: 6 g

Spinach and Broccoli Quiche

Number of Servings: 6

Ingredients:

- 15 oz. chopped spinach
- 16 oz. firm tofu
- ¾ cup diced broccoli
- ¼ cup and 1 Tbsp. soy milk
- 1 ½ Tbsp. coconut aminos
- 1 ½ tsp. Dijon mustard
- 1 ½ tsp. dried parsley
- ¾ tsp. dried rosemary
- ¾ tsp. garlic powder
- Freshly ground black pepper, to taste

For the Crust:

- 1 ¼ cups whole wheat flour
- 1 ¼ cups all-purpose flour
- ½ cup chilled nut butter

How to Prepare:

Preheat the oven to 350 degrees F to preheat.

First make the crust by combining the whole wheat and all purpose flour in a bowl. Add the nut butter and cut it into the mixture until crumbly, adding just enough ice cold water to create a dough.

Press the dough onto a pie pan and refrigerate.

Combine the spinach and broccoli in a saucepan and add just enough water to cover the base. Cover the saucepan and place over high flame. Bring to a boil, then turn off the heat and set aside to steam.

Meanwhile, combine the tofu, coconut aminos, soy milk, Dijon mustard, garlic powder, parsley, rosemary, and a pinch of black pepper in a food processor and blend until combined.

Drain the spinach and broccoli, pressing out as much water as possible. Combine the tofu mixture with the spinach and broccoli then spread in the prepared pie crust.

Bake for 30 minutes, or until the mixture is golden brown and the crust is cooked.

Transfer to a cooling rack and let cool slightly. Slice into equal wedges then serve.

Nutritional Information per Serving:

240 grams per 1 serving

Energy (calories): 444 kcal

Protein: 23 g

Fat: 19 g

Carbohydrates: 51 g

Savory Broccoli Omelet

Number of Servings: 2

Ingredients:

- 2 garlic cloves

- 2 organic eggs

- 4 organic egg whites

- ¾ cup chopped broccoli

- ¼ cup crumbled low-fat feta cheese

- 2 Tbsp. avocado, grape seed, or sunflower oil

- Chili pepper flakes, to taste

- Freshly ground black pepper, to taste

How to Prepare:

Crush the garlic cloves with the handle of your knife and peel off the skins. Mince well then set aside.

Whisk the eggs and egg whites in a bowl then set aside.

Place a large nonstick skillet over medium flame then add 1 tablespoon of the oil. Swirl to coat.

Sauté the chopped broccoli until crisp tender then stir in the garlic and sauté until fragrant. Season lightly with chili pepper flakes and black pepper. Mix well then transfer into a bowl and set aside.

Wipe the skillet clean with paper towels and reheat over low flame. Whisk the eggs one more time then pour into the skillet. Tilt the pan to distribute the eggs and let them cook evenly.

Once partially firm, flip over the egg and then spread the broccoli mixture on half of it. Add the feta cheese on top. Cover the skillet and cook for about 30 seconds, then remove from heat and transfer the omelet to a platter. Slice into three servings and serve right away.

Nutritional Information per Serving:

185 grams per 1 serving

Energy (calories): 347 kcal

Protein: 21 g

Fat: 27 g

Carbohydrates: 3 g

Chapter 3 – DASH Main Dish Recipes

Mushroom and Three-Herb Pesto Whole Wheat Fettuccine

Number of Servings: 4

Ingredients:

- 1 onion
- 1 lb. large mushrooms, such as oyster
- 8 oz. dried fettuccine pasta
- 6 oz. kale
- 3 garlic cloves
- ¾ cup vegetable broth, low or no sodium
- ½ cup fresh parsley leaves
- 1/3 cup freshly grated Parmesan cheese
- 3 Tbsp. olive oil
- 2 ½ Tbsp. chopped walnuts
- ¾ tsp. minced fresh rosemary
- Freshly ground black pepper, to taste

How to Prepare:

Peel and chop the onions then set aside. Slice the large mushrooms in half then set aside.

Prepare the fettuccine based on package instructions.

Meanwhile, peel the garlic cloves and place them in a food processor. Add the walnuts, parsley, thyme, and rosemary. Process until finely minced. Add 2 tablespoons of olive oil and blend again until smooth. Set aside.

In the boiling pasta water, add the kale and cook until tender. Drain the pasta and kale, saving ¾ cup of the pasta water. Set aside.

Place a saucepan over medium flame and heat the remaining olive oil. Sauté the onion and mushrooms until tender. Add the herb pesto and stir well to coat. Simmer until the liquid is reduced by half.

Add the pasta and kale into the mushroom sauce and toss well to coat. Season to taste with black pepper.

Divide the pasta into four servings and top with Parmesan cheese. Serve right away.

Nutritional Information per Serving:

316 grams per 1 serving

Energy (calories): 465 kcal

Protein: 11 g

Fat: 15 g

Carbohydrates: 77 g

Thai Inspired Quinoa Salad

Number of Servings: 3

Ingredients:

- 1 small red bell pepper
- 1 small carrot
- 2 cups homemade vegetable broth, low or no sodium
- 1 cup raw quinoa
- ½ cup shelled edamame
- 2 ½ Tbsp. chopped green onion
- 1 Tbsp. chopped fresh Thai basil
- ½ Tbsp. extra virgin olive oil
- ¾ tsp. chopped fresh mint
- ½ tsp. sesame seeds
- Chili pepper flakes, to taste
- Freshly ground black pepper, to taste

How to Prepare:

Pour the quinoa into a fine mesh strainer and rinse thoroughly under cold running water until the water runs clear. Drain well then transfer into a saucepan.

Stir the vegetable broth into the quinoa, then cover the pot and place over high flame. Bring to a boil, then reduce to low flame and simmer for 8 to 10 minutes, or until the quinoa is tender. Fold in the shelled edamame, then cover the pot and set aside for 5 minutes.

Meanwhile, peel the carrot and grate using the large holed grater. Stem, core, and seed the bell pepper then chop into tiny bits. Set aside.

After 5 minutes, uncover the pot and fluff up the quinoa. The edamame should be crisp tender as well. Transfer everything into a large bowl and fold in the carrot, bell pepper, green onion, Thai basil, olive oil, fresh mint, and sesame seeds. Mix well.

Season to taste with chili pepper flakes and black pepper, then divide into three servings and serve right away, or cover, refrigerate and serve chilled.

Nutritional Information per Serving:

280 grams per 1 serving

Energy (calories): 274 kcal

Protein: 11 g

Fat: 6 g

Carbohydrates: 44 g

Onion and Potato Stuffed Herring

Number of Servings: 3

Ingredients:

- 1 small onion
- 1 garlic clove
- 3 whole herring, 4 oz. Each
- 3 small red potatoes
- 3 Tbsp. chopped fresh flat leaf parsley
- ¾ tsp. olive oil
- White vinegar, to taste
- Onion powder, to taste
- Freshly ground black pepper, to taste

How to Prepare:

Place the red potatoes into a pot and add enough water to cover. Cover the pot then place over high flame. Bring to a boil, then reduce to a simmer and let simmer for 10 minutes, or until the potatoes are fork tender.

Drain the potatoes then peel and slice thinly.

Set the oven to 400 degrees F to preheat.

Clean and rinse the herrings thoroughly then slice in half lengthwise.

Peel and mince the onion and garlic then divide them among the herrings. Divide the potatoes among the herrings then drizzle with olive oil. Top with parsley.

Season with onion powder, black pepper, and sprinkle with white vinegar. Close the herrings then wrap each herring with aluminum foil, sealing tightly.

Arrange the herrings in a baking sheet and bake for 30 minutes.

Carefully remove from the oven and remove the aluminum foil. Serve the stuffed herring with white vinegar.

Nutritional Information per Serving:

433 grams per 1 serving

Energy (calories): 299 kcal

Protein: 9 g

Fat: 3 g

Carbohydrates: 63 g

Tomato Basil Penne Pasta

Number of Servings: 3

Ingredients:

- 3 cups whole wheat penne pasta
- 1 ¼ cups halved cherry tomatoes
- 1 cup chopped fresh basil
- ¾ cup sliced fresh mozzarella cheese
- 1 ½ Tbsp. extra virgin olive oil
- 2 ½ Tbsp. toasted pine nuts
- Garlic powder, to taste
- Freshly ground black pepper, to taste

How to Prepare:

Cook the penne pasta according to package instructions. Drain thoroughly and transfer to a bowl.

Add the mozzarella cheese to the hot pasta and gently toss until the cheese is melted. Fold in the cherry tomatoes and basil then season to taste with garlic powder and black pepper.

Drizzle in the olive oil and sprinkle in the toasted pine nuts. Toss well until combined. Divide into three servings and serve right away.

Nutritional Information per Serving:

128 grams per 1 serving

Energy (calories): 387 kcal

Protein: 20 g

Fat: 10 g

Carbohydrates: 59 g

Baked Lemon Trout with Almonds and Green Beans

Number of Servings: 6

Ingredients:

- 6 whole trout fillets, 5 oz. Each

- 3 lb. green beans

- 1 lemon

- 1/3 cup thinly sliced almonds

- 6 Tbsp. olive oil

- 1 ½ Tbsp. freshly squeezed lemon juice

- 1 ½ Tbsp. chopped fresh flat leaf parsley

- Freshly ground black pepper, to taste

How to Prepare:

Set the oven to 400 degrees F to preheat. Line a baking sheet with parchment paper and set aside.

Boil a pot of water over high flame. Once boiling, add the green beans and blanch for 1 minute. Drain immediately and rinse under cold running water.

Transfer the green beans to a bowl and add the freshly squeezed lemon juice. Toss well to coat then season with black pepper and set aside.

Spread the sliced almonds on the prepared baking sheet and bake in the oven for about 3 minutes, or until lightly golden brown and toasted. Immediately transfer to a cooling rack and set aside.

Rinse the trout fillets thoroughly then blot dry with paper towels. Lightly oil with some of the olive oil then season with black pepper all over.

Arrange the trout on a baking sheet. Slice the lemon thinly and arrange on top of the trout fillets. Bake for 10 minutes, or until cooked through.

Carefully place the trout on a platter and top with the parsley. Serve right away with the green beans.

Nutritional Information per Serving:

401 grams per 1 serving

Energy (calories): 412 kcal

Protein: 33 g

Fat: 26 g

Carbohydrates: 12 g

Grilled Pepper Tuna Steaks with Spicy Apple and Black Bean Salad

Number of Servings: 3

Ingredients:

- 3 tuna steaks, 3 oz. each
- 1 Granny Smith apple
- 1 small red onion
- 1 ½ cups cooked or canned black beans, low sodium
- ½ Serrano chili pepper
- 3 Tbsp. freshly squeezed lime juice
- 1 ½ Tbsp. chopped fresh cilantro
- Freshly ground black pepper

How to Prepare:

Halve the Granny Smith apple and scoop out and discard the core. Slice into tiny cubes and place into a bowl. Add the lime juice to prevent browning and toss gently to coat. Set aside.

Peel and dice the red onion then add into the bowl of apple. Rinse and drain the black beans thoroughly then add into the bowl as well. Seed and dice the

Serrano chili pepper then add into the bowl, followed by the cilantro. Toss everything to combine. Cover the bowl and refrigerate for 1 hour.

Meanwhile, preheat the grill to medium high.

Rinse the tuna steaks then blot dry with paper towels. Season both sides with black pepper then grill for about 4 minutes per side, or until cooked through.

Transfer the tuna steaks into serving plates. Take the salad out of the refrigerator and spoon next to each grilled tuna steak. Serve right away.

Nutritional Information per Serving:

303 grams per 1 serving

Energy (calories): 329 kcal

Protein: 25 g

Fat: 16 g

Carbohydrates: 21 g

Greek Inspired Chicken Waldorf

Number of Servings: 3

Ingredients:

- 1 small apple
- ¾ cup sliced grapes
- 1 ½ cups chopped cooked boneless, skinless chicken
- ¾ cup chopped celery
- 1/3 cup chopped toasted walnuts
- 4 ½ Tbsp. low fat plain Greek yogurt
- 1 ½ Tbsp. olive oil
- 1 ½ tsp. freshly squeezed lemon juice

How to Prepare:

Combine the yogurt, lemon juice, and olive oil, then set aside.

In a salad bowl, combine the chicken, grapes, celery, and 3 tablespoons of chopped walnuts.

Core and dice the apple then fold into the chicken mixture. Add the yogurt mixture then toss gently to coat. Top with the remaining walnuts then serve right away.

Nutritional Information per Serving:

154 grams per 1 serving

Energy (calories): 188 kcal

Protein: 3 g

Fat: 13 g

Carbohydrates: 17 g

_____

Ginger and Lime Sea Bass

Number of Servings: 3

Ingredients:

- 1 small onion

- 1 garlic clove

- 3 sea bass fillets, 5 oz. each

- 1 ½ lb. chopped leafy greens, such as spinach, kale, or chard

- 1/3 cup freshly squeezed lime juice

- 1 ½ Tbsp. minced fresh flat leaf parsley

- ¾ Tbsp. olive oil

- ¾ Tbsp. raw honey

- ¾ tsp. fresh rosemary

- Freshly ground black pepper, to taste

How to Prepare:

Steam the greens until tender, then remove from heat and press out the excess water. Chop and place in a bowl. Add about ¼ cup of lime juice and toss well to coat. Set aside.

Rinse the sea bass fillets then blot dry with paper towels. Set aside.

Place a nonstick skillet over medium flame and heat through. Add the olive oil and swirl to coat. Add the sea bass fillets and cook for 3 minutes per side, or until browned. Add about 3 tablespoons of lime juice then cover and reduce to low flame. Simmer for about 5 minutes or until the fillets are cooked through. Transfer to a platter and set aside.

Stir the garlic, onion, ginger, raw honey, rosemary, and remaining lime juice in the skillet. Bring to a boil, then reduce to a simmer. Simmer until the sauce is thickened slightly.

Strain the sauce then spoon over the fillets. Top the sea bass fillets with parsley and serve with steamed greens.

Nutritional Information per Serving:

374 grams per 1 serving

Energy (calories): 20 kcal

Protein: 10 g

Fat: 10 g

Carbohydrates: 24 g

Vegetable Angel Hair Pasta

Number of Servings: 3

Ingredients:

- 1 small onion
- 1 garlic clove
- 1 small green bell pepper
- 6 oz. raw angel hair pasta
- 1 ½ cups diced Roma tomatoes
- 1 ½ cups chopped fresh zucchini
- ¾ cup chopped mushrooms
- 3 Tbsp. chopped olives
- 1 ½ Tbsp. shredded Parmesan cheese
- 3 tsp. olive oil
- Freshly ground black pepper, to taste

How to Prepare:

Prepare the angel hair pasta following the package instructions.

Meanwhile, dice the tomatoes and set aside. Peel and dice the onion and garlic then set aside. Chop the onions and set aside.

Place a saucepan over medium flame and heat through. Once hot, add the olive oil and swirl to coat.

Sauté the onion until translucent then add the garlic and sauté until fragrant. Add the green bell pepper, mushrooms, and zucchini and sauté until crisp tender.

Stir in the tomatoes with their juices and simmer until cooked through.

Drain the pasta thoroughly then fold in the vegetable and sauce. Divide into three servings, top with Parmesan cheese, and serve right away.

Nutritional Information per Serving:

215 grams per 1 serving

Energy (calories): 168 kcal

Protein: 4 g

Fat: 7 g

Carbohydrates: 24 g

Turkey Tacos

Number of Servings: 3

Ingredients:

- 4 corn tortillas, 6 inches each
- 3 radishes
- 1 small white onion
- 1 garlic clove
- 1 small red bell pepper
- 1/3 lb. extra lean minced or ground turkey
- ½ cup chopped tomatoes
- 3 Tbsp. chopped fresh cilantro
- 1 ½ Tbsp. avocado, grape seed, or sunflower oil
- 1 Tbsp. freshly squeezed lime juice
- ½ tsp. dried oregano
- ¼ tsp freshly ground black pepper
- ¼ tsp. chili pepper flakes

How to Prepare:

Peel and mince the white onion and garlic clove then set aside.

Stem, core, and seed the bell pepper then chop into tiny bits and set aside.

Peel and thinly slice the radishes then set aside.

Combine about 2 tablespoons of the chopped white onion into a bowl, then add the chopped tomatoes with their juices, cilantro, lime juice, and a pinch of the chili pepper flakes. Mix well and set aside.

Place a large skillet over medium high flame and add the oil. Sauté the remaining onion until translucent, then stir in the bell pepper and sauté until tender. Stir in the garlic and sauté until fragrant.

Add the turkey and sauté until browned all over, breaking the meat into bits. Season with the dried oregano and black pepper then mix well.

Place a nonstick skillet over medium flame and warm the tortillas on both sides. Place the tortillas on three plates. Divide the turkey mixture among them, followed by the tomato salsa mixture. Top with radishes and the fold up and secure with toothpicks, if needed. Serve right away.

Nutritional Information per Serving:

497 grams per 1 serving

Energy (calories): 277 kcal

Protein: 15 g

Fat: 10 g

Carbohydrates: 35 g

Mediterranean Style Baked Mackerel and Mushrooms

Number of Servings: 6

Ingredients:

- 6 mackerel, 6 oz. Each
- 6 Roma tomatoes
- 2 garlic cloves
- 2 lemons
- 12 oz. white mushrooms
- 3 Tbsp. minced fresh flat leaf parsley
- 3 Tbsp. herbes de Provence
- 1 Tbsp. Dijon mustard
- Freshly ground black pepper, to taste

How to Prepare:

Set the oven to 400 degrees F to preheat.

Rinse the mackerel thoroughly then blot dry with paper towels. Season the mackerel, including the cavity, with black pepper.

Cut out six sheets of aluminum foil, each sheet large enough to cover one mackerel.

Slice the lemon thinly and divide into six equal portions. Slice the tomatoes and divide them into six equal portions as well.

Peel and mince the garlic then set aside.

Lay one mackerel on top of each sheet of aluminum foil then add the mushrooms on top, followed by lemon and tomato slices. Spoon the Dijon mustard on top, followed by the mushrooms and parsley. Sprinkle with herbes de Provence.

Seal the aluminum foil, crimping the edges tightly. Arrange the wrapped mackerel on a baking sheet and bake for 25 minutes.

Once the mackerel are ready, carefully remove from the oven. Remove the aluminum foil and serve right away.

Nutritional Information per Serving:

367 grams per 1 serving

Energy (calories): 220 kcal

Protein: 37 g

Fat: 4 g

Carbohydrates: 8 g

Baked Herbed Red Snapper

Number of Servings: 3

Ingredients:

- 1 small onion
- 1 garlic clove
- 3 red snapper fillets, 5 oz. each
- 3 Roma tomatoes
- 1 cup chopped artichoke hearts
- 1 ½ Tbsp. chopped fresh flat leaf parsley
- 1 ½ Tbsp. chopped fresh basil
- 1 ½ tsp. chopped fresh oregano
- 1 ½ tsp. chopped fresh thyme
- 2 tsp. olive oil
- Freshly ground black pepper, to taste

How to Prepare:

Set the oven to 400 degrees F to preheat.

Chop the tomatoes and set aside with their juices. Peel and mince the onions then set aside.

Rinse the fillets then blot dry with paper towels and season with black pepper on both sides. Set aside.

Place a skillet over medium frame and heat through. Add the olive oil and swirl to coat. Sauté the onion until translucent then stir in the garlic and sauté until fragrant. Add the tomatoes, fresh herbs and artichokes then sauté until tender. Season to taste with black pepper.

Spread half vegetable mixture on the baking pan and lay the red snapper fillets. Add the remaining vegetable mixture on top.

Cover the baking pan and bake for 18 minutes, or until the fillets are cooked through.

Transfer to a cooling rack and let stand for 5 minutes. Serve warm.

Nutritional Information per Serving:

341 grams per 1 serving

Energy (calories): 226 kcal

Protein: 33 g

Fat: 5 g

Carbohydrates: 12 g

Tex Mex Chicken and Avocado

Number of Servings: 3

Ingredients:

- 3 boneless, skinless chicken breasts
- 6 corn tortillas
- 1 avocado
- 1 large bell pepper
- 1 large green bell pepper
- 1 large yellow bell pepper
- 1 small white onion
- 1 large garlic
- 2 ½ Tbsp. low fat plain Greek yogurt
- 2 ½ Tbsp. water
- 2 Tbsp. olive oil
- 2 Tbsp. freshly squeezed lemon juice
- ½ tsp. dried oregano
- Ground cumin, to taste
- Ground cayenne, to taste
- Freshly ground black pepper, to taste

How to Prepare:

Halve the avocado and discard the stone. Scoop out the flesh and place inside a bowl or food processor. Add the yogurt, water, lemon juice, and a pinch of black pepper, cumin, and cayenne, or to taste. Mash or blend until smooth, then set aside.

Rinse the chicken breasts thoroughly then blot dry with paper towels. Slice into thin strips then season with black pepper, cumin, and some of the oregano. Set aside.

Stem, core, and seed the bell peppers. Chop into thin strips and set aside. Peel and dice the onion and garlic then set aside.

Place a saucepan over medium high flame and heat through. Once hot, add the oil and swirl to coat. Add the chicken and cook for about 5 minutes, or until browned all over.

Add the bell peppers, onion, and garlic then sauté until the bell peppers are tender and the onion is translucent. Season with the remaining oregano and black pepper. Transfer to a bowl and set aside.

Place a nonstick skillet over medium low flame and warm the tortillas. Divide the tortillas into three servings then heap the chicken and vegetable mixture on top. Spoon the avocado dressing on top then serve right away.

Nutritional Information per Serving:

346 grams per 1 serving

Energy (calories): 567 kcal

Protein: 19 g

Fat: 29 g

Carbohydrates: 63 g

Spiced Eggplant Stew

Number of Servings: 3

Ingredients:

- 9 baby eggplants
- 1 small sweet onion
- 3 garlic cloves
- 2 ½ cups chopped tomatoes
- ¾ cup low fat plain Greek yogurt
- ¼ cup chopped fresh cilantro
- 1 ½ Tbsp. chopped fresh mint
- 2 ¼ Tbsp. olive oil
- 1 ½ tsp. ground cumin
- 1 ½ tsp. ground coriander
- 2 ½ tsp. raw honey
- Chili pepper flakes, to taste
- Freshly ground black pepper, to taste

How to Prepare:

Peel and mince the garlic and onion then set aside.

Slice the baby eggplants in half lengthwise and set aside.

Place a saucepan over medium high flame and heat through. Add ½ tablespoon of olive oil and swirl to coat.

Add the baby eggplants in a single layer then add 1 ½ teaspoons of raw honey and all the cumin, coriander, and a pinch of chili pepper flakes on top. Stir until combined and the eggplants are tender.

Add the tomatoes with the juices and stir well. Cover, reduce to medium low flame, and simmer for 10 to 15 minutes, or until the sauce is thickened slightly and the eggplant is tender.

Meanwhile, combine the yogurt, half of the cilantro, all of the mint, olive oil, and remaining honey in a food processor. Blend until smooth.

After the eggplant stew is done, add the remaining cilantro and season with black pepper.

Divide the eggplant stew into three servings and spoon the sauce on top. Serve right away.

Nutritional Information per Serving:

788 grams per 1 serving

Energy (calories): 788 kcal

Protein: 42 g

Fat: 23 g

Carbohydrates: 121 g

Savory Veggie Chili

Number of Servings: 4

Ingredients:

- 1 small red onion
- 2 garlic cloves
- 1 small avocado
- 2 zucchinis
- 1 small red bell pepper
- 15 oz. canned black beans, low or no sodium
- 7.5 oz. canned chickpeas, low or no sodium
- 7.5 oz. canned kidney beans, low or no sodium
- 1 cup chopped tomatoes
- ½ cup homemade vegetable broth, low or no sodium
- 4 Tbsp. low-fat plain Greek yogurt
- 2 Tbsp. chopped fresh cilantro
- 1 ½ Tbsp. olive oil
- ½ Tbsp. chili powder
- ¼ tsp. ground cumin
- ¼ tsp. dried parsley

- ¼ tsp. dried basil

- ¼ tsp dried oregano

- Freshly ground black pepper, to taste

How to Prepare:

Peel and dice the red onion and garlic cloves then set aside. Chop the zucchinis and set aside. Stem, core, and seed the bell pepper then dice and set aside.

Rinse the black beans, chickpeas, and kidney beans in cold running water and drain thoroughly. Set aside.

Place a stock pot over medium high flame and add the olive oil. Stir in the red onion and sauté until translucent. Add the garlic and sauté until fragrant. Then, stir in the zucchini and bell pepper and sauté until crisp tender.

Pour in the vegetable broth and stir in the black beans, chickpeas, and kidney beans. Add the chopped tomatoes with their juices, followed by the chili powder, ground cumin, and dried herbs. Mix everything well.

Simmer over medium-low flame, loosely covered, for about 30 minutes or until the chili is slightly thickened. Remove from heat and set aside.

Halve the avocado and discard the stone. Scoop out the flesh and slice into bite-sized cubes. Set aside.

Divide the chili into three servings and add the avocado on top. Spoon the yogurt over the avocado then garnish with the fresh cilantro. Serve right away.

Nutritional Information per Serving:

386 grams per 1 serving

Energy (calories): 328 kcal

Protein: 14 g

Fat: 17 g

Carbohydrates: 33 g

Chapter 4 – DASH Side Dish Recipes

Zucchini Spinach Soup

Number of Servings: 3

Ingredients:

- 1 small onion

- 1 small zucchini

- 7.5 oz. canned cannellini beans

- 2 cups baby spinach

- 1 cup homemade vegetable broth, low or no sodium

- 1 cup water

- 1 Tbsp. freshly squeezed lemon juice

- ¾ Tbsp. olive oil

- 2 tsp. minced fresh mint leaves

- 1 tsp. freshly grated lemon zest

- Freshly ground black pepper, to taste

How to Prepare:

Peel and minced the onion then set aside. Dice the zucchini and set aside.

Rinse and drain the cannellini beans thoroughly then set aside.

Place a saucepan over medium flame and heat through. Once hot, add the olive oil and swirl to coat.

Sauté the onion until translucent then stir in the zucchini and sauté until crisp tender.

Pour in the vegetable broth and water, then increase to high flame and bring to a boil. Once boiling, reduce to a simmer and add the beans and spinach.

Reduce to medium low flame and simmer for 3 minutes, or until the spinach is wilted.

Turn off the heat then stir in the mint, lemon juice, and zest. Season to taste with black pepper and serve right away.

Nutritional Information per Serving:

283 grams per 1 serving

Energy (calories): 116 kcal

Protein: 11 g

Fat: 5 g

Carbohydrates: 9 g

Mediterranean Pomegranate, Avocado and Pear Salad

Number of Servings: 3

Ingredients:

- 1 Anjou pear
- 1 small avocado
- 3 cups arugula
- ½ cup thinly sliced fennel
- 3 Tbsp. pomegranate seeds
- 1 Tbsp. freshly squeezed lemon juice

How to Prepare:

Halve the pear then remove the core. Slice the pear as thinly as possible then place in a salad bowl.

Halve the avocado and discard the stone. Scoop out the flesh and slice into small, bite-sized cubes. Add to the bowl of sliced pear.

Sprinkle the lemon juice over the pear and avocado to prevent browning and toss gently to coat. Set aside.

Divide the arugula into three servings and lay the sliced fennel on top. Divide the pear and avocado mixture among the servings then top with pomegranate seeds. Serve right away.

Nutritional Information per Serving:

175 grams per 1 serving

Energy (calories): 159 kcal

Protein: 2 g

Fat: 10 g

Carbohydrates: 18 g

Potato, Leek, and Bean Stew

Number of Servings: 4

Ingredients:

- 1 small white onion
- 1 leek
- 2 potatoes
- 2 cups homemade vegetable broth, no or low sodium
- ½ cup cannellini beans
- ½ cup low fat milk
- ¼ Tbsp. olive oil
- Freshly ground black pepper, to taste
- Dried rosemary, to taste
- Dried thyme, to taste

How to Prepare:

Peel the potato and dice into tiny cubes. Set aside. Rinse the cannellini beans thoroughly in cold running water then drain thoroughly.

Rinse and trim the leek then thinly slice and set aside.

Peel and mince the white onion and set aside.

Place a soup pot over medium flame and heat through. Once hot, add the olive oil and swirl to coat. Sauté the onion until translucent then add the leek and sauté until tender.

Stir in the diced potatoes until tender then stir in the beans and vegetable broth. Bring to a boil then reduce to simmer. Simmer until the potatoes are tender but not soggy.

Stir in the milk, then season to taste with black pepper, rosemary, and thyme. Mix well.

Ladle into soup bowls and serve right away.

Nutritional Information per Serving:

415 grams per 1 serving

Energy (calories): 247 kcal

Protein: 9 g

Fat: 2 g

Carbohydrates: 50 g

Warm Potato and Spinach Salad

Number of Servings: 3

Ingredients:

- 12 oz. baby red potatoes
- 6 oz. green beans
- 5 cups baby spinach leaves
- 1/3 cup chopped green onions
- 3 Tbsp. white vinegar
- 3 Tbsp. chopped fresh flat leaf parsley
- 3 Tbsp. olive oil
- 1 ½ Tbsp. fresh dill
- Garlic powder, to taste
- Freshly ground black pepper, to taste

How to Prepare:

Trim the green beans and chop into bite-sized pieces. Set aside.

Place the baby potatoes into a pot and add enough water to cover by about an inch. Cover the pot, place over high flame, and bring to a boil. Once boiling, reduce to a simmer and cook for about 6 minutes, or until the potatoes are fork tender.

Add the green beans into the pot and simmer for 1 minute or until crisp tender. Drain everything and set aside in a colander.

Place a skillet over medium flame and heat through. Once hot, stir in the green onion and sauté until just tender. Transfer to a bowl then pour in the vinegar. Stir to combine.

Place the green beans and potatoes into a bowl and add the olive oil and green onion and vinegar mixture. Toss well to coat then sprinkle in the parsley and dill. Season to taste with garlic powder and black pepper.

Divide the baby spinach into three servings then heap the warm potato mixture on top of each. Serve right away.

Nutritional Information per Serving:

269 grams per 1 serving

Energy (calories): 241 kcal

Protein: 5 g

Fat: 15 g

Carbohydrates: 25 g

Grilled Garlic and Lemon Asparagus

Number of Servings: 3

Ingredients:

- 1 lb. asparagus

- 2 garlic cloves

- 3 Tbsp. olive oil

- 2 Tbsp. freshly squeezed lemon juice

- 1 tsp. freshly grated lemon zest

- Garlic powder, to taste

- Freshly ground black pepper, to taste

How to Prepare:

Preheat the grill.

Crush the garlic cloves with the handle of a knife and peel off the skins. Finely mince the garlic and set aside.

Trim the asparagus spears, discarding the tough ends. Arrange the asparagus spears on a baking sheet and drizzle with olive oil. Toss to coat.

Add the lemon juice to the asparagus spears and toss again to coat. Season with the lemon zest, minced garlic, garlic powder, and black pepper.

Grill the asparagus spears for about 2 minutes, basting with the oil on the baking sheet, until crisp tender.

Transfer the grilled asparagus on a platter and serve right away.

Nutritional Information per Serving:

179 grams per 1 serving

Energy (calories): 155 kcal

Protein: 4 g

Fat: 14 g

Carbohydrates: 7 g

Minty Cranberry Wild Rice Salad

Number of Servings: 3

Ingredients:

- 1 ¼ cups cooked wild rice
- 2 ½ Tbsp. olive oil
- 1 ½ Tbsp. freshly squeezed orange juice
- ¾ Tbsp. raw honey or pure maple syrup
- ½ Tbsp. freshly grated orange zest
- 3 Tbsp. pine nuts
- 3 Tbsp. dried cranberries
- 3 Tbsp. minced fresh mint
- 1 ½ Tbsp. chopped green onion
- 1 ½ tsp. Dijon mustard
- Freshly ground black pepper, to taste

How to Prepare:

Combine the orange juice and zest, honey or maple syrup, and Dijon mustard. Whisk well to combine.

Fold the rice into the sauce with the mint, pine nuts, cranberries, and green onion. Season to taste with black pepper then serve right away.

Nutritional Information per Serving:

116 grams per 1 serving

Energy (calories): 199 kcal

Protein: 3 g

Fat: 11 g

Carbohydrates: 22 g

Broccoli Soup

Number of Servings: 3

Ingredients:

- 6 cups chopped broccoli florets
- 1 small white onion
- 1 large garlic clove
- 1 ½ cups homemade vegetable broth, low or no sodium
- 1/3 cup low fat milk
- 1 Tbsp. olive oil
- Freshly ground black pepper, to taste
- Chili pepper flakes, to taste

How to Prepare:

Peel and chop the onion and garlic then set aside.

Place the chopped broccoli florets into a pot and add enough water to cover it halfway. Cover and place over high flame then bring to a boil. Once boiling, reduce to low flame and simmer for 3 to 4 minutes, or until the broccoli florets are fork tender.

Drain the broccoli and rinse in cold running water. Set aside.

Place a pot over medium flame and heat through. Once hot, add the olive oil and swirl to coat. Sauté the onion until translucent, then add the garlic and sauté until fragrant.

Add the broccoli and stir well to combine. Then, pour in the vegetable broth and bring to a boil. Once boiling, reduce to simmer until the vegetables are fork tender but not soggy.

Turn off the heat then blend the mixture with an immersion blender until smooth.

Stir in the low fat milk then season to taste with black pepper and chili pepper flakes. Mix well then ladle into soup bowls and serve piping hot.

Nutritional Information per Serving:

230 grams per 1 serving

Energy (calories): 78 kcal

Protein: 3 g

Fat: 5 g

Carbohydrates: 5 g

Brown Rice Pilaf

Number of Servings: 3

Ingredients:

- 1 small onion

- 1 small carrot

- 1 small red bell pepper

- 1 garlic clove

- 1 cup homemade vegetable broth, low or no sodium

- ½ cup brown rice

- ¾ Tbsp. minced fresh flat leaf parsley

- ¾ tsp. olive oil

- Freshly ground black pepper, to taste

How to Prepare:

Peel and mince the onion and garlic then set aside. Peel the carrot and dice. Core, seed, and dice the bell pepper then set aside.

Rinse the rice thoroughly then drain. Set aside.

Place a saucepan over high flame and heat through. Once hot, add the olive oil and swirl to coat. Sauté the onion until translucent then add the garlic and sauté until fragrant.

Add the bell pepper and sauté until tender then add the rice and sauté until combined. Add the vegetable broth and parsley, then bring to a boil.

Once boiling, reduce to low flame, cover, and cook for 20 minutes, or until the rice is tender and has absorbed the vegetable broth.

Season to taste with black pepper then transfer to a bowl. Serve right away.

Nutritional Information per Serving:

164 grams per 1 serving

Energy (calories): 202 kcal

Protein: 13 g

Fat: 3 g

Carbohydrates: 31 g

Herbed Roasted Butternut Squash Soup

Number of Servings: 3

Ingredients:

- 1 small garlic clove

- 1 small white onion

- 8 oz. chopped butternut squash

- 3 cups homemade vegetable broth, low or no sodium

- 1 ½ Tbsp. olive oil

- ½ Tbsp. chopped fresh flat leaf parsley

- ½ tsp. chopped fresh rosemary

- 2 fresh sage leaves, minced

- Freshly ground black pepper, to taste

- Chili pepper flakes, to taste

How to Prepare:

Set the oven to 400 degrees F to preheat.

Spread the chopped butternut squash on a roasting pan and drizzle with 1 tablespoon of olive oil. Toss well to coat then roast for 15 to 20 minutes, or until tender. Transfer to a cooling rack and set aside.

Place a soup pot over medium flame and heat through. Once hot, add the remaining olive oil and swirl to coat. Sauté the onion until translucent then add the garlic and sauté until fragrant.

Stir in the butternut squash and sauté until coated in the onion and garlic mixture. Then, add the broth and stir well to combine. Bring to a boil, then reduce to low flame, cover, and simmer until squash is tender.

Blend the soup with an immersion blender until smooth. Then, season to taste with the black pepper and chili pepper flakes. Stir in the fresh herbs, then ladle into soup bowls and serve piping hot.

Nutritional Information per Serving:

318 grams per 1 serving

Energy (calories): 107 kcal

Protein: 0.8 g

Fat: 7 g

Carbohydrates: 12 g

Ginger Quinoa Bowl

Number of Servings: 3

Ingredients:

- 1 small onion
- 1 small apple
- ¾ cup vegetable juice
- ½ cup quinoa
- ½ cup frozen peas
- 2 ½ Tbsp. chopped toasted almonds
- 2 ½ Tbsp. shredded unsweetened coconut flakes
- 1 Tbsp. minced fresh ginger
- 1 tsp. avocado, grape seed, or sunflower oil
- Freshly ground black pepper, to taste

How to Prepare:

Peel and dice the onion and set aside.

Rinse the quinoa thoroughly and set aside.

Place a saucepan over medium flame. Add the oil and sauté the onion until translucent. Add the ginger, vegetable juice, and quinoa. Mix well then season with black pepper.

Increase to high flame and bring to a boil. After that, reduce to low flame and simmer for 10 minutes or until the quinoa has completely absorbed the liquids.

Turn off the heat and fold the peas into the quinoa. Cover and let stand for 3 minutes or until the peas are cooked.

Meanwhile, core the apple then dice and set aside.

Divide the quinoa into three servings and fold in the toasted almonds, shredded coconut flakes, and diced apple. Serve right away.

Nutritional Information per Serving:

205 grams per 1 serving

Energy (calories): 270 kcal

Protein: 6 g

Fat: 13 g

Carbohydrates: 34 g

Cauliflower and Carrot Soup

Number of Servings: 3

Ingredients:

- 1 Tbsp. olive oil
- 1 small white onion
- 1 large garlic clove
- 1 small carrot
- 4 cups chopped cauliflower florets
- 2 cups homemade vegetable broth, low or no sodium
- Freshly ground black pepper, to taste
- Chili pepper flakes, to taste
- Dried basil, to taste

How to Prepare:

Peel and chop the onion and garlic then set aside. Peel and dice the carrot and set aside.

Place the chopped cauliflower florets into a pot and add enough water to cover it halfway. Cover and place over high flame then bring to a boil. Once boiling, reduce to low flame and simmer for 3 to 4 minutes, or until the cauliflower is fork tender.

Drain the cauliflower and rinse in cold running water. Set aside.

Place a pot over medium flame and heat through. Once hot, add the olive oil and swirl to coat. Sauté the onion until translucent, then add the garlic and sauté until fragrant. Add the carrot and sauté until crisp tender, then add the cauliflower and mix well.

Pour the vegetable broth into the pot then bring to a simmer. Blend everything with an immersion blender then season to taste with black pepper, chili pepper flakes, and dried basil.

Ladle into soup bowls and set aside.

Nutritional Information per Serving:

322 grams per 1 serving

Energy (calories): 92 kcal

Protein: 3 g

Fat: 5 g

Carbohydrates: 11 g

Chilled Lentil Thyme Salad

Number of Servings: 3

Ingredients:

- 1 garlic clove
- ½ lb. Lentils
- 1 bay leaf
- 3 Tbsp. extra virgin olive oil
- 1 ½ Tbsp. chopped fresh thyme
- 1 Tbsp. wine vinegar
- ½ Tbsp. minced shallot
- ½ tsp. Dijon mustard
- Garlic powder, to taste
- Freshly ground black pepper, to taste

How to Prepare:

Rinse the lentils thoroughly then place them into a small pot. Add just enough water to cover them completely, then place over high flame, cover, and bring to a boil.

Once boiling, reduce to a simmer and cook for 30 minutes, or until the lentils are almost tender.

Meanwhile, crush and peel the garlic and set aside.

Whisk together the wine vinegar, Dijon mustard, and shallot. Gradually whisk in the olive oil then season to taste with black pepper. Set aside.

Once the lentils are done, drain them and place in a large bowl. Add enough water until the lentils are covered by about an inch, then add the garlic and bay leaf. Cover and boil over high flame. Once boiling, reduce to low flame and simmer for 10 minutes.

Drain the lentils and discard the bay leaf. Transfer the lentils into a bowl and fold in the dressing. Mix well then cover and refrigerate for at least 30 minutes, or until chilled. Best served chilled.

Nutritional Information per Serving:

100 grams per 1 serving

Energy (calories): 140 kcal

Protein: 7 g

Fat: 6 g

Carbohydrates: 18 g

Kale, Carrot, and Sweet Potato Soup

Number of Servings: 3

Ingredients:

- 2 garlic cloves
- 1 small yellow onion
- 1 large carrot
- 1 large sweet potato
- 2 cups homemade vegetable broth, low or no sodium
- 1 cup chopped kale
- ¾ cup cooked or canned cannellini beans
- ½ cup chopped tomatoes
- 1 Tbsp. olive oil
- ¼ tsp. dried oregano
- ¼ tsp. chopped fresh thyme
- Chili pepper flakes, to taste

How to Prepare:

Peel and dice the garlic and onion then set aside. Peel and dice the carrot and sweet potatoes, then set aside.

Place a soup pot over medium flame and heat through. Once hot, add the olive oil and swirl to coat. Sauté the onion until translucent, then add the garlic and sauté until fragrant.

Stir in the carrot and sweet potato then sauté until crisp tender. Stir in the oregano and a pinch of chili pepper flakes, or to taste. Mix well then pour in the vegetable broth, tomatoes with their juices, and the fresh thyme.

Cover and bring to a boil. Once boiling, reduce to medium low flame and cook for about 5 minutes.

Meanwhile, rinse and drain the beans thoroughly. After that, stir into the pot with the kale. Cook until the sweet potatoes are fork tender.

Ladle into soup bowls and serve piping hot.

Nutritional Information per Serving:

316 grams per 1 serving

Energy (calories): 130 kcal

Protein: 2 g

Fat: 5 g

Carbohydrates: 20 g

Split Pea and Carrot Soup

Number of Servings: 3

Ingredients:

- 1 small onion
- 1 large garlic clove
- 2 small carrots
- 1 celery stalk
- 3 cups homemade vegetable broth, low or no sodium
- 1 cup yellow or green split peas
- 1 bay leaf
- ½ tsp. dried thyme
- Freshly ground black pepper, to taste

How to Prepare:

Peel and chop the onion then set aside. Peel and dice the carrots and celery stalk and set aside.

Rinse and drain the split peas thoroughly then place in a soup pot. Add the vegetable broth, then stir in the garlic, diced carrot and celery, bay leaf, and dried thyme.

Cover and place over high flame then bring to a boil. Once boiling, reduce to a simmer and cook for 25 to 30 minutes, or until the split peas are cooked through.

Season to taste with the black pepper and ladle into soup bowls. Serve right away.

Nutritional Information per Serving:

364 grams per 1 serving

Energy (calories): 268 kcal

Protein: 16 g

Fat: 0.8 g

Carbohydrates: 51 g

South American Summer Salad

Number of Servings: 3

Ingredients:

- 3 Roma tomatoes
- 1 small white onion
- 3 cups chopped romaine lettuce
- ¾ cup sliced cucumber
- 2 ½ Tbsp. freshly squeezed lime juice
- Extra virgin olive oil, to taste
- Onion or garlic powder, to taste
- Freshly ground black pepper, to taste

How to Prepare:

Peel and thinly slice the white onion, then place in a salad bowl. Chop the Roma tomatoes and place into the bowl with the onion. Add the romaine lettuce, and sliced cucumber. Toss well to combine.

Pour the lime juice and add a drizzle of olive oil over the salad. Season with a pinch of onion or garlic powder and black pepper. Toss well to combine.

Divide into three servings and serve right away.

Nutritional Information per Serving:

172 grams per 1 serving

Energy (calories): 29 kcal

Protein: 2 g

Fat: 0.3 g

Carbohydrates: 6 g

Chapter 5 – DASH Dessert Recipes

Warm Cinnamon Apricots

Number of Servings: 3

Ingredients:

- 3 large apricots
- ¾ Tbsp. olive oil
- Ground cinnamon, to taste

How to Prepare:

Preheat the grill.

Halve the apricots and discard the stones. Lightly coat the apricot halves with the olive oil and place on the hot grill. Grill for about 3 minutes per side, or until tender.

Transfer the hot apricot halves on a platter and sprinkle with cinnamon on top. Let stand for about 5 minutes, then serve. Alternatively, chill for about 30 minutes before serving.

Nutritional Information per Serving:

168 grams per 1 serving

Energy (calories): 109 kcal

Protein: 2 g

Fat: 4 g

Carbohydrates: 18 g

Dark Chocolate Banana Yogurt Bowls

Number of Servings: 3

Ingredients:

- 3 small bananas
- 1 ½ cups low fat plain Greek yogurt
- 1/3 cup sliced strawberries
- 4 ½ Tbsp. chopped dark chocolate
- 3 Tbsp. chopped unsalted pistachios or cashews

How to Prepare:

Put the dark chocolate into a microwaveable bowl and microwave for about 10 seconds, or until melted. Stir well and set aside.

Peel the bananas and slice each in half lengthwise. Place each split banana into a bowl then divide the yogurt among the three servings.

Drizzle the dark chocolate on top of the banana and yogurt then top with sliced strawberries and chopped nuts. Serve right away.

Nutritional Information per Serving:

257 grams per 1 serving

Energy (calories): 272 kcal

Protein: 10 g

Fat: 10 g

Carbohydrates: 40 g

Minty Fruit Salad

Number of Servings: 3

Ingredients:

- 1 banana
- 1 small apple
- ½ cup water
- ¼ cup sliced strawberries
- ¼ cup fresh blueberries
- ¼ cup fresh raspberries
- 2 Tbsp. pomegranate seeds
- 1 ½ Tbsp. chopped fresh mint leaves
- ¾ Tbsp. freshly squeezed lemon juice
- ¾ Tbsp. raw honey

How to Prepare:

Pour the water into a small saucepan and bring to a boil. Once boiling, turn off the heat and stir in the raw honey, lemon juice, and mint leaves. Set aside to steep then strain and transfer into the refrigerator to cool.

Before serving, peel the banana and slice into thin pieces. Place into a bowl. Core the apple and dice then add to the bowl of banana. Add the strawberries, blueberries, and raspberries.

Add the chilled lemon mint tea into the salad and toss to combine. Top with pomegranate seeds and serve right away.

Nutritional Information per Serving:

203 grams per 1 serving

Energy (calories): 125 kcal

Protein: 1 g

Fat: 0.3 g

Carbohydrates: 32 g

Hearty Oatmeal Raisin Cookies

Number of Servings: 18 pieces

Ingredients:

- 1 large egg
- 1 ½ cups traditional rolled oats
- ½ cup whole wheat flour
- ½ cup raisins
- ½ cup toasted chopped walnuts
- ¼ cup raw honey or pure maple syrup
- ¼ cup nut butter, at room temperature
- 1 ½ Tbsp. flaxseeds
- ½ tsp. baking soda
- ½ tsp. pure vanilla extract
- ¼ tsp. ground cinnamon
- Ground ginger, to taste
- Ground nutmeg, to taste

How to Prepare:

Set the oven to 350 degrees F to preheat.

Meanwhile, combine the raw honey or pure maple syrup with the nut butter and mix well until smooth and creamy.

Add the vanilla extract and egg then blend well to combine. Set aside.

In another bowl, combine the whole wheat flour, flaxseeds, baking soda, cinnamon, and a pinch of ginger and nutmeg. Mix well.

Gradually fold the flour mixture into the egg mixture until smooth. Fold in the oats, walnuts, and raisins then mix well.

Spoon the batter onto a dry baking sheet making sure there is enough space between each.

Bake for 8 minutes, or until the cookies are golden brown. Transfer to a cooling rack and allow to cool for about 5 minutes. Serve warm or store in an airtight container for up to 1 week.

Nutritional Information per Serving:

23 grams per 1 piece

Energy (calories): 86 kcal

Protein: 3 g

Fat: 5 g

Carbohydrates: 12 g

Berry Yogurt Bowls

Number of Servings: 3

Ingredients:

- 1 ½ cups low fat plain Greek yogurt
- ¾ cup fresh blueberries
- ¾ cups fresh raspberries
- ¾ cup sliced fresh strawberries
- 3 Tbsp. chopped toasted almonds
- 1 ½ Tbsp. freshly squeezed orange juice
- ¼ tsp. pure vanilla extract

How to Prepare:

Place the berries in a bowl with the orange juice and vanilla extract. Toss well to combine.

Divide the yogurt into three servings then divide the berry mixture on top of each. Top with chopped toasted almonds then serve right away.

Nutritional Information per Serving:

296 grams per 1 serving

Energy (calories): 215 kcal

Protein: 8 g

Fat: 3 g

Carbohydrates: 42 g

Conclusion

Hopefully this book has spurred you to take action and implement the DASH diet today. As you can see, it is neither expensive nor time-consuming to prepare your own meals especially if you consider the tremendous health benefits of doing so.

Just remember to make your meals ahead of time with the best quality ingredients your budget allows. This is best achieved when you have a meal plan to guide you on what to serve and eat during particular times.

Also take note that variety is the key to a delicious meal. By making a variety of small dishes and then storing them in the refrigerator, you can serve at least three different flavors – a main dish and two easy small dishes – in each meal. That way, mealtimes will be so festive you will embrace the DASH diet for the rest of your life!

Continue reading, and you will find 5 more recipes!

Preview of DASH diet: 77 Recipes

Introduction

I want to thank you and commend you for downloading the book, *"Dash Diet: 77 Delicious Dash Diet Recipes with an Easy Guide for Rapid Weight Loss"*.

This book contains 77 delicious, easy-to-make recipes for effective and sustainable weight loss with easy-to-understand guidelines.

Your days of trying on diet after diet after diet are finally over!

When done correctly, the DASH diet can help you lose weight and lower your blood pressure in as early as two weeks. However, contrary to what the name may suggest, the DASH diet is not a speedy starve-yourself-for-a-week trick. No, it doesn't follow the old pattern of deprivation, craving, and that sad slippery slide back to unhealthy eating habits. And ultimately, this is what makes this weight reduction plan successful.

Your first step towards successful *and* sustainable weight loss is to view DASH as more than just a diet but as a choice. It is an important and conscious choice that you make day after day and meal after meal.

Why just aspire for a fit body when you can also aim for a healthy heart? Through this book, you will gain a deeper understanding of the DASH diet, its countless benefits, and where and how you should begin.

The reason why most weight loss diets fail is because they are often incompatible with most people's lifestyles. Inevitably, dieters end up crawling back to the same old unhealthy eating pattern that has always worked for their household and their busy schedules. The great thing about the recipes found in this book is that they are simple and easy to prepare. They don't require exotic ingredients from "special" diet stores.

This diet doesn't require isolating yourself from others during mealtime. In fact, you'll find that these healthy, mouth-watering meals are designed to be incorporated into your daily routine with as little inconvenience and as much gastronomic pleasure as possible!

Thanks again for downloading this book, I hope you enjoy it!

Chapter 1 - The DASH Diet and Guidelines for Rapid Weight Loss

What is the DASH Diet?

The DASH Diet is a clever acronym for Dietary Approaches to Stop Hypertension. Despite the fact that this weight loss program has gained massive popularity throughout the years, it wasn't initially designed as a reducing diet. In fact, the main objective of the DASH diet is to lower blood pressure, thus, lessening your risk of developing a broad array of diseases. That said, significant weight loss is a pleasant side effect. This means that with the DASH diet, not only will you get the figure that you want; you can also achieve the best level of health that you deserve.

Why should you Switch to this Diet?

One of the most obvious benefits of the DASH diet is a healthy heart. This diet will boost good cholesterol while booting the bad cholesterol. Individuals who suffer from moderate hypertension will experience noticeable improvements even without medication.

Furthermore, this diet lessens your risk for developing diseases linked with high blood pressure and obesity. Research reveals that the DASH diet helps diabetics to manage their condition effectively,

Since the DASH is low in calorie, it will inevitably lead you to shed excess fat especially when coupled with moderate exercise. This doesn't have to be strenuous exercise, but just enough physical activity to steer clear of a sedentary lifestyle.

Another thing that sets the DASH diet apart from most reducing diets out there is that it focuses on satiety, thus, reducing your need to eat more frequently than you should and ensuring that your brain and body functions at their maximum capacity all throughout the day.

Studies also show that this diet reduces your risk for developing cancer, bone diseases and psychological illnesses.

Another reason why this reducing diet has long-term potential is the absence of any health risks. Furthermore, DASH dieters also swear to its anti-aging side effects.

What Foods are you Allowed to Eat?

The heart of this life-changing diet lies in consuming a huge chunk of plant-based foods such as vegetables and fruits while consuming moderate amounts of zero fat to low fat dairy. Beans, seeds and nuts are allowed. Though the latter gained a bad rep for being rich in fat, nuts have omega 3 fatty acids that contribute to a healthy heart. You may incorporate almonds, peas, pistachio, lentils, and sunflower seeds into your diet. You may also eat fish, poultry and lean meat.

The DASH diet is a low sodium diet. It is high in fiber and moderate in fat. Another thing you need to remember when following this diet is to stay away from empty carbohydrates, such as white bread (which is a common item in most grocery carts) and other refined and processed edibles. You have to replace them with whole wheat bread and healthy grains that you also need to take in moderation. Like any other sensible weight loss diet, the DASH diet encourages cutting the consumption of sweets and calorie-rich edibles.

DASH diet is all about *sustainable* weight loss. When it comes to snacks, they should be substantial and rich in protein and heart-friendly fats. This lessens the occurrence of cravings. The fact that the DASH diet consists of considerable amounts of proteins ensures that you can maintain muscle, even as you shed weight. This prevents your metabolism from slowing.

What are this Diet's Nutritional Goals?

You need to meet the following requirements on a daily basis:

- Daily sodium intake must be a minimum of 1,500 mg and a maximum of 2,300 mg.

- Total fat should be 27 % of calories with saturated fat consisting 6 % of calories.

- 18% of calories must be from protein.

- Meanwhile, carbohydrates are 55% of calories.

- Have at least 30 g fiber daily.

- Lastly, but most importantly, limit cholesterol to 150 mg per day.

How Much should you Eat?

When it comes to grains, you may eat six up to eight servings per day. One slice of bread or ½ cup of cereal is equivalent to one serving. That said, consume more high-fiber, nutrient-rich whole grains like barley, steel cut oats, quinoa and buckwheat, and avoid refined grains. When shopping, study the label and opt for food items that have 100% whole wheat or 100% whole grain.

Four to five servings of fruits, such as grapefruits, bananas, plums, grapes, kiwi fruit, mangoes, and prunes are recommended. A 4 oz. glass of fruit juice or a medium-sized fruit is considered as one serving. When eating fruits like apples and pears, consider eating the peel as well because it's where you'll find the highest levels of fiber and antioxidants. Beware of added sugars in canned fruit juices.

As for vegetables, it is advisable to eat four to five servings daily of potassium-rich and magnesium-rich green leafy veggies, sweet potatoes, eggplant, celery, tomatoes, butternut squash, carrots, parsnips and other root vegetables. Note that when doing your grocery shopping, fresh and organic is the way to go. If you *must* settle for canned varieties, always opt for brands with the lowest sodium content.

Milk and dairy products like goat cheese, low fat cottage cheese and low fat sour cream are great sources of protein, calcium and Vitamin D in the DASH diet. The recommended daily serving is two to three. Always opt for low fat varieties as opposed to whole milk products.

Meat like turkey, beef and pork tenderloin are not prohibited since this is where you'll get some of your protein and B complex vitamins. That said, you need to restrict your consumption to two servings daily of lean and skinned meat. Wild-caught fish, like salmon and tuna, are preferable to red meat.

As mentioned, you may safely and *occasionally* snack on seeds, beans and nuts like cashews, pistachios, pecans and pumpkin seeds. That said, the recommended intake is four to five servings per week. Contrary to what some may think, it is not advisable to scratch off fat from the diet. It enables you to absorb essential vitamins to support your immune system. In the DASH diet, fat intake is restricted to a maximum of 27%. This means you need to limit yourself to two to three daily servings. A serving is equivalent to one teaspoon of margarine or two teaspoon of salad dressing.

Recommended beverages include 100% fruit juice, herbal tea and low-sodium vegetable soup. That said, the best is plain water.

It's alright to use condiments, like bean dip, hummus, fresh salsa, pesto and balsamic vinegar. When buying mayonnaise, go for the low fat variety. When shopping for fruit spreads, choose ones with low sugar content.

The good news is you don't have to cry over saying goodbye to sweets. You can still eat low fat cookies, fruit ice pops, granola bars and other desserts in this book as long as you limit them to a maximum of five servings per week. Not too bad, all in all.

Chapter 2 - A Healthy Start: The DASH Breakfast

DASH Pancakes

Ingredients:
- 1 cup flour (whole wheat)

- 8 oz milk (1%)

- 3 eggs, organic

- 1 banana

- 2 tbsp walnuts

- 2 tsp olive oil

- 1 tsp vanilla

- 1/4 tsp salt

- 1 tsp baking powder

- ¼ tsp cinnamon

Instructions:
1. Mash the bananas, then chop the nuts.

2. Separate the egg whites from the yolk then set the yolks aside.

3. In a mixing bowl, combine all dry ingredients.

4. In a separate bowl, pour the milk then add the vanilla, the banana, and the egg whites. Mix well.

5. Use a handheld mixer to combine the wet and dry ingredients to form a batter.

6. Adjust the stove to medium setting and heat a non-stick pan after mildly greasing it with cooking spray.

7. Pour 2 oz batter onto the pan for each pancake.

8. Once you achieve a mildly browned color and firm texture on one side, flip the pancake over.

9. Dig in!

Easy DASH Omelet

Ingredients:
- 8 eggs, organic
- 2 tbsp chives
- 4 oz cheddar cheese (reduced fat)
- 2 cups spinach leaves, torn and steamed
- 1/8 tsp salt
- Pepper as desired

Instructions:
1. Mildly grease a non-stick pan with cooking spray then heat it.
2. Meanwhile, whisk the eggs along with the chives, cheese, salt and pepper.
3. Pour the mixture into the pan.
4. Use a wooden spatula to toss the eggs continuously until they are cooked. This will take approximately 45 seconds.
5. Finally, top your omelet with the spinach for a more filling breakfast.

Note: This recipe serves 4 persons.

DASH Tofu Scramble

Ingredients:
- 18 oz tofu (extra firm)
- 2 tomatoes, deseeded and chopped
- 2 poblano peppers, deseeded and chopped
- 1 tbsp olive oil
- ½ tsp cumin, ground
- Juice from ½ lime
- ½ tsp dehydrated oregano
- 2 garlic cloves, minced
- 1 tsp chili powder
- ¼ tsp salt

Instructions:
1. Drain the water from the tofu then slice it into half. Afterwards, use a paper towel to pat it dry.
2. Crush the tofu to small pieces.
3. Grease a non-stick pan with the olive oil and heat it.
4. Sauté the garlic, onion and pepper for about 5 minutes.
5. Add the other spices.
6. Cook for an extra ½ minute.

7. Next, add the tofu. Cook it for 5 minutes.

8. Just when it's almost ready, pour in the lime juice then throw in the tomatoes.

9. Enjoy your scrambled egg substitute!

DASH Breakfast Smoothie

Ingredients:
- 1 banana, medium-sized

- 8 oz baby spinach

- 4 oz non-fat milk

- 2 oz plain yogurt

- 6 oz mango slices, frozen overnight

- ¼ cup steel cut oats

- ½ tsp vanilla

Instructions:
1. First, mix the oats, the milk and the yogurt together in a blender for 15 seconds. Select the high setting.

2. Add the mango, the banana, the spinach, and the vanilla.

3. Blend well until you get a smooth texture.

4. Drink up!

DASH Breakfast Crunch

Ingredients:
- ½ cup granola cereal or muesli, low fat
- 1 cup grapefruit or orange, sliced
- 1 cup apple, sliced
- 1 cup seedless grapes
- 1 cup kiwi, sliced
- 12 oz vanilla yogurt, low fat
- 2 tbsp raw wild honey

Instructions:
1. In a bowl, combine all the fruits then sprinkle the yogurt on top of them.
2. Sprinkle granola on top.
3. Pour some honey to add more sweetness.

Note: Serves 4-6

Check out this book.

Check out more books by Celine Walker!

Made in the USA
San Bernardino, CA
15 July 2017